GW00992533

Chapter 1: Social Media

Chapter 2: Gaming

Chapter 3: Digital Detox

Introduction

Online Safety is Volume 409 in the **issues** series. The aim of the series is to offer current, diverse information about important issues in our world, from a UK perspective.

Online Safety

Over half of the world's population has a social media account. With billions of people using social media, we need to know how to stay safe online. This book explores social networking – the positives and the negatives as well as ways to stay savvy and recognise online risks.

OUR SOURCES

Titles in the **issues** series are designed to function as educational resource books, providing a balanced overview of a specific subject.

The information in our books is comprised of facts, articles and opinions from many different sources, including:

♦ Newspaper reports and opinion pieces

♦ Website factsheets

♦ Magazine and journal articles

♦ Statistics and surveys

♦ Government reports

♦ Literature from special interest groups.

A NOTE ON CRITICAL EVALUATION

Because the information reprinted here is from a number of different sources, readers should bear in mind the origin of the text and whether the source is likely to have a particular bias when presenting information (or when conducting their research). It is hoped that, as you read about the many aspects of the issues explored in this book, you will critically evaluate the information presented.

It is important that you decide whether you are being presented with facts or opinions. Does the writer give a biased or unbiased report? If an opinion is being expressed, do you agree with the writer? Is there potential bias to the 'facts' or statistics behind an article?

ASSIGNMENTS

In the back of this book, you will find a selection of assignments designed to help you engage with the articles you have been reading and to explore your own opinions. Some tasks will take longer than others and there is a mixture of design, writing and research-based activities that you can complete alone or in a group.

FURTHER RESEARCH

At the end of each article we have listed its source and a website that you can visit if you would like to conduct your own research. Please remember to critically evaluate any sources that you consult and consider whether the information you are viewing is accurate and unbiased.

Useful Websites

www.ditchthelabel.org

www.healthforteens.co.uk

www.independent.co.uk

www.inews.co.uk

www.kidscape.org.uk

www.metro.co.uk

www.ofcom.org.uk

www.openaccessgovernment.org

www.parentzone.org.uk

www.shropshirestar.com

www.theconversation.com

www.theguardian.com

www.thinkuknow.co.uk

www.uswitch.com

www.voicebox.site

Online Safety

Editor: Danielle Lobban

Volume 409

Exeter School Library

WITHDRAWN

300450858

independence
educational publishers

First published by Independence Educational Publishers

The Studio, High Green

Great Shelford

Cambridge CB22 5EG

England

© Independence 2022

Copyright

This book is sold subject to the condition that it shall not,
by way of trade or otherwise, be lent, resold, hired out or otherwise
circulated in any form of binding or cover other than that in which it
is published without the publisher's prior consent.

Photocopy licence

The material in this book is protected by copyright. However, the
purchaser is free to make multiple copies of particular articles for instructional
purposes for immediate use within the purchasing institution.
Making copies of the entire book is not permitted.

ISBN-13: 978 1 86168 868 2

Printed in Great Britain

Zenith Print Group

The rise of social media: how the world became connected

By Daniel Morris

W hen his catchy number 'Without Me' was released back in 2002, Mr Marshall Bruce Mathers III (A.K.A. Eminem) probably didn't think that in only a couple of years the rest of the world would be calling for followers at the top of their lungs too.

Twenty years later, the reach, impact and overall influence of social media are almost inescapable.

In the decade in which we sit, colossal portions of our lives are lived online. True, the pandemic and the restrictions that accompanied it have played a part in increasing the amount that we live through the internet. Yet even so, much of global society had already long been on course for the level of 'web world' that now dominates our daily existence.

A tool for both work and play, the net is an incredible resource that in modern society we would now almost doubtlessly be lost without. Yet over the last 20 years particularly, it has become the vehicle for such a gargantuan proportion of our social activity that for many it is now seen as integral to their interaction with others.

Social media in all of its forms has indisputably changed the world. In the positive, it has connected people personally and professionally, given friends and loved ones another avenue of long-distance contact, and brought people from all corners of the planet together in discussion of interests, advancement of causes and debate over views.

In the negative, it has provided a platform for those who would callously abuse, belittle, intimidate, bully and hurt others to do so from behind the shield of anonymity, and verbally attack anyone, at any time, from any place.

Though it has brought both good and bad to global society, what cannot be denied is that social media is now a cog without which the machine of the modern world would struggle to function.

Here, we take a look at its fascinating growth, the birth and rise of some of the most popular platforms, and the mind-blowing grip social media as a whole currently has on over half of the planet's population.

Ah, when all we needed was MySpace and MSN, eh? Alas, they would come to be only a drop in the ocean...

The history bit: development of social-media platforms

Though the complex history of social media and its genesis goes back quite a bit further, SixDegrees, launched in 1997, is often regarded as the first real online social networking site.

The development of social media began with simple platforms such as GeoCities – one of the earliest social networking services – which was launched in 1994, followed by Classmates.com in 1995, and then SixDegrees two years later.

Unlike instant-messaging services that did not feature personal profiles and the like, SixDegrees was the first online site that was created for 'real people', using their real names and including friends lists and school affiliations. Little did its makers know that social media would one day come to drive the lives of the planet...

Fast-forward to 2015 (and following the launch and growth of some pretty big names in the social media sphere) research showed that the people of the world spent 22 per cent of their online time on social networks, their popularity having skyrocketed due to the widespread love affair with the smartphone.

In 2021, 4.33 billion people worldwide were using social media. That's a lot. A very lot indeed...

Some of the most popular social media sites of today (and when we say 'popular', we mean those with more than a whopping 100 million registered users) include TikTok, WeChat, Instagram, QZone, Tumblr, LinkedIn, Weibo, Twitter and, of course, the big daddy of them all, Facebook. Depending on interpretation, other platforms that are referred to as social media services include YouTube, Quora, Snapchat, Pinterest, and WhatsApp.

Over half the world connected...

To repeat, there are 4.33 billion active social media users worldwide. In context, the world's population is currently sat at around 7.9 billion, and you don't have to be much of maths whizz to figure out that that means more than half the people on God's green Earth are social media users. According to DataReportal, there were 409 million new users on social media in the month of October 2021 alone.

The pandemic has certainly played its part in a recent boost in social media users. Between October 2019 and October 2020, social network usage reportedly grew by a whopping 21.3%.

Holding ourselves to account...

As of last year, the average 18 to 34-year-old was running 8.4 profiles on social media. In India, that average was 11.5.

Such numbers make you wonder how we find the time to actually socialise. However, multi-social media use is quite easily explained through the fact that many platforms that can technically be described as 'social media' are specialised services used by many users for one specific purpose – Instagram for photos, LinkedIn for work, YouTube for videos, etc.

Even so, where do we find the time to run our online selves?

Getting down to business...

Reportedly, 81 per cent of small and medium-sized enterprises (SMEs) have social media accounts, with companies allocating an average of 14 to 20 per cent of their marketing budget to social media.

At the last check, 71 per cent of SMEs were marketing their wares or services via social media, and of this number, 52 per cent were creating a marketing post at least once a day.

There's no denying that these days it's a big part of what keeps the money machine turning...

The platforms to end all platforms (and we don't mean heels)...

Facebook

The indisputable Goliath of the whole bunch, with roughly 2.91 billion monthly active users as of the third quarter of 2021, Facebook is the biggest social network worldwide.

As a business, Meta Platforms Inc owns Facebook, WhatsApp, Instagram and Messenger. As such, during the first quarter of 2021, 3.45 billion people were reportedly visiting at least one of its core products.

A name now almost synonymous with internet use, Facebook is the third most visited website in the world with an estimated 3.65 billion monthly visits, only being outranked by YouTube at 3.99 billion and Google at a colossal 17.37 billion.

Despite having come into the world way back in the murky days of the early noughties, Facebook is still one of the most downloaded apps on the planet. Indeed, by the close of 2020, only TikTok had trumped

Facebook in terms of the number of total downloads that year.

On average, users spend 34 minutes on Facebook every day. This may not sound like that much, but that's 238 minutes a week (just shy of four hours) and 12,376 minutes a year (over eight-and-a-half full days).

Twitter

With 199 million monetisable daily active users, Twitter continues to pack a punch in the social media pantheon.

Interestingly, according to recent stats, people aged between 35 and 49 make up the largest demographic of Twitter users – 28.4 per cent of the total usage population. However, they are followed hot on their heels by the 25 to 34s, who comprise 26.6 per cent of the network's user base.

On average, a rather sizeable 500 million tweets are shared per day. This works out at 6,000 tweets per second, 350,000 tweets per minute, and a whopping 200 billion tweets every year.

While the average Twitter user has just over 700 followers, it is of course possible to garner quite a few more than this, and all the easier if you're one of them there famous types. Christiano Ronaldo is packing an impressive 92.1 million, and Justin Bieber is doing even better at 114.4 million.

But alas, both are falling short in comparison to Barack Obama, who is leading the pack with a mighty 130.3 million followers.

Ah, to be popular...

Instagram

This photo-driven behemoth of a platform is flying high these days, at last count boasting a total of 1.074 billion active monthly users.

Instagram crossed the 1 billion line back in 2018, and as part of the Meta empire, is a mighty cog in a seemingly unstoppable machine.

Interestingly, 88 per cent of Instagram users are in fact outside the US, though the country does still boast 140 million account holders.

The sixth most visited website in the world, there are more than 200 million business accounts on Instagram, and over 500 million accounts use Instagram Stories every single day.

They say a picture paints a thousand words, and in turns out a lot of people agree...

LinkedIn

Built to help people forge professional connections, LinkedIn now has more than 756 million users in over 200 countries.

Naturally, the majority of users are employed professionals, or graduates seeking work, and with this in mind it's no great surprise that the 25s to 34s make up the biggest user demographic, representing a chunky 60.1 per cent of those with personal accounts. Currently there are over 57 million companies listed on LinkedIn along with around 15 million job openings.

A big sell with this platform is that it allows the publication of long-form content, as well as images, short text and videos, and this is undoubtedly responsible for a big part of its continued popularity in the business world.

TikTok

With an impressive 850 million downloads in 2020, the triumphant video-focused TikTok became that year's most popular social media platform.

Having picked up the pace in terms of users in 2019 (in fact crossing the 1 billion line that year), TikTok's popularity became meteoric as the Covid pandemic progressed, proving a huge lockdown hit. Initially targeting users aged 18 and under, TikTok has now become popular with adults and at least 9 in 10 users open the app on a daily basis.

Today, TikTok is available in 155 countries and can be accessed in 75 languages. Although it's still quite a new kid on the block in terms of the social media scene, TikTok has spent the last couple of years proving it is a force to be reckoned with, banking $1 billion in 2020 alone.

As it stands today, the company is worth over $50 billion. Yikes.

18 February 2022

The above information is reprinted with kind permission from the Shropshire Star.
© 2022 Shropshire Star

www.shropshirestar.com

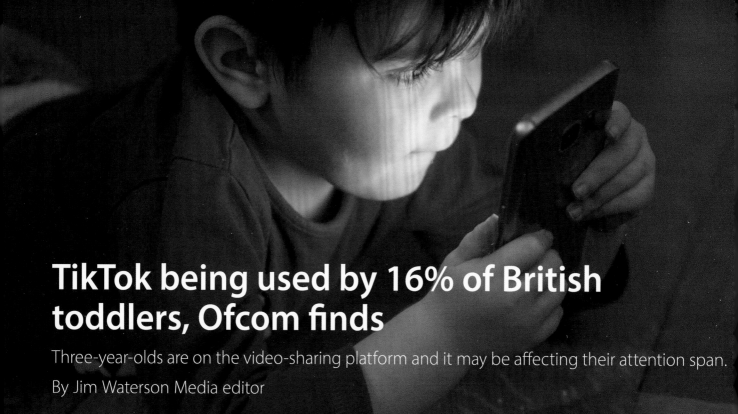

TikTok being used by 16% of British toddlers, Ofcom finds

Three-year-olds are on the video-sharing platform and it may be affecting their attention span.

By Jim Waterson Media editor

British toddlers are increasingly likely to be users of TikTok, with a substantial number of parents saying their preschool children use the video service despite the app supposedly being restricted to those aged 13 and older.

About 16% of three- and four-year-olds view TikTok content, according to research commissioned by media regulator Ofcom. This rises to a third of all children in the five- to seven-year-old age group.

TikTok's terms of service excludes under-13s and its moderators have instructions to look out for content produced by younger users and to block their accounts. However, the research suggests the age checks on new users are being widely flouted.

The reality that young children – often aided by parents creating profiles or sharing their mobile phone – are accessing TikTok could cause regulatory headaches for the company. Its powerful recommendation algorithm has helped it grow into one of the most powerful media platforms in the world, but it is undergoing the same growing pains that have affected platforms such as Facebook and YouTube, with concerns about content covering topics such as eating disorders and adult material.

Since it began being enforced last year, the UK's age-appropriate design code has required British apps and websites with large numbers of child users to pay particular attention to the personal data they are gathering on young users and to provide a higher level of privacy by default. But the code has no specific restrictions for very young children.

A TikTok spokesperson said: "Nothing is more important to us than the safety of our community, especially young people.

TikTok is strictly a 13-plus platform and we have processes in place to enforce our minimum age requirements, both at the point of sign up and through the continuous proactive removal of suspected underage accounts from the platform."

Ofcom's annual survey of the nation's media habits also suggested the growing popularity of short-form content could be linked to multiscreening, with more children reporting difficulties in focusing on a single online activity. Children reported being unable to watch films, or other long-form content, without being on multiple devices at the same time. Only 4% of children aged three to 17 said they never do anything else while watching television.

The number of British households without access to the internet has remained at about 1.7m – equivalent to 6% of British homes. The vast majority in this category are older people or those on the lowest incomes, with most saying they have no plans to go online in the next year – even though that increasingly leaves them cut off from many services and forms of communication.

There are also signs that Britons are less tolerant of online anonymity and more concerned that something they posted online could come back to haunt them later in life. Ofcom found that 55% of Britons now disagree with the idea that people should be able to say whatever they want online, even if hurtful or controversial, up from 47% in 2020.

29 March 2022

The above information is reprinted with kind permission from *The Guardian*.
© 2022 Guardian News and Media Limited

www.theguardian.com

Boys and girls feel negative effects of social media, at different ages

Girls experience the negative effects of social media use aged 11-13, while boys feel this later at 14-15 – scientists find teens who use social media more, have a lower life satisfaction.

Girls are often more vulnerable to the negative effects of social media use at an earlier age than boys, yet both are at risk at different age groups of being less satisfied in life with too much social media use.

UK data shows, girls experience a negative link between social media use and life satisfaction when they are 11-13 years old and boys when they are 14-15 years old.

Negative effects of social media use can involve bullying, comparison, body dysmorphia, depression, anxiety, distraction, and can often generate an unrealistic perception of one's life.

The negative effects of social media use can be linked to developmental changes in teenagers, where changes in the structure of the brain or changes during puberty may be experienced with obsessive use – however, this has been found to occur later in boys than in girls.

Pinpointing which individuals might be more influenced by social media

Possible social changes – such as leaving home or starting work – may make people more vulnerable to excessive social media use. As social media has fundamentally changed how young people spend time, this has led to widespread concern about its potential negative impact.

According to research published today by the Oxford Internet Institute, in a study published in Nature Communications, researchers analysed two UK datasets comprising some 84,000 individuals between the ages of 10 and 80 years old.

Including longitudinal data – data that tracks individuals over a period of time – on 17,400 young people aged 10-21 years old, they found that social media use at the age of 19 years was again associated with a decrease in life satisfaction.

Though there is still considerable uncertainty about how social media relates to wellbeing, researchers looked for a connection between estimated social media use and reported life satisfaction, and found important periods of adolescence where social media use was associated with a subsequent decrease in life satisfaction.

Teens who have lower than average life satisfaction later use more social media

The researchers aim to further look at social media use effects and encourage conversations from parents, schools, governments and social media companies to develop a better understanding of what drives these changes across the age groups and between genders.

Dr Amy Orben, from the University of Cambridge, who led the study, said: "The link between social media use and mental wellbeing is clearly very complex. Changes within our bodies, such as brain development and puberty, and in our social circumstances appear to make us vulnerable at particular times of our lives.

"I wouldn't say that there is a specific age group we should all be worried about. We should all be reflecting on our social media use and encouraging those conversations but we need to understand what is driving these changes across the age groups and between genders.

"There are very large individual differences, so there may be certain teenagers that benefit from their use of social media whilst at the same time, someone else is harmed."

Dr Orben added: "With our findings, rather than debating whether or not the link exists, we can now focus on the periods of our adolescence where we now know we might be most at risk and use this as a springboard to explore some of the really interesting questions.

"It's not about social media being good or bad, it's about what young people are up to, why they are using it, and how they feel about it fits into the greater picture of family life."

The researchers call on social media companies to share their data with independent scientists, and for governments to tackle online harms by introducing legislation to compel these companies to be more open.

28 March 2022

The above information is reprinted with kind permission from Open Access Government.
© 2022 Adjacent Digital Politics LTD

www.openaccessgovernment.org

Why social media and screen time can be bad for children, but rarely as bad as parents fear

The link between screen time and mental health is not as clear as we think.

By Tom Chivers

Every modern parent has the 'screen time' worry.

It's hard not to feel guilty when you put your toddler in front of an iPad so you can get some washing done, or let them watch endless loops of bizarre YouTube videos of someone playing with Thomas the Tank Engine toys or Elsa dolls.

My own kids are slightly older, and now the concern has morphed into how long the eight-year-old spends playing Fifa on the Switch or whether the Disney+ princess programmes the six-year-old stares at are age-appropriate.

This does not, as I understand it, get easier with time. At least our children are still too young to have seriously started demanding phones of their own. But it will not be long, in the grand scheme of things, before they are using TikTok or whatever has succeeded it by then to interact with their friends. 'Social media', a catch-all term for everything from WhatsApp, DM groups to YouTube, is a central part of modern adolescence.

And in recent years, there has been growing concern that screen time is harming young people's mental health. Social media, in particular, worries parents: whether it's by creating a new avenue for children to bully each other, or by presenting unrealistic images of happy lives and perfect bodies.

Every so often, widely publicised studies come out that seem to find worrying trends – studies that, for instance, find that 'depression, self-harm, suicide and unhappiness' all increased dramatically in US adolescents, especially girls and young women, after 2012. That study explicitly links the rise to social media.

These fears have led to all sorts of reactions, from major articles with headlines like 'Have Smartphones Destroyed a Generation?' to Sunday Times investigations suggesting that social media is behind a rise in teen suicides. In 2018, the then Health Secretary, Matt Hancock, even compared the risk of social media to the well-established dangers of eating too much sugar. Worries like this are partly behind legislation like the Online Harms Bill, currently working its way through parliament.

But what's been difficult has been getting good scientific evidence that screen time in general, or social media in particular, are causing these harms. So the field has been left open to speculation and fear mongering.

This week a study came out in the journal *Nature Communications*. It tried to answer some questions that parents and others will have about what effect social media has, if any, on adolescents' mental health, and looking to see if there are times when young people are especially vulnerable.

It found what appears to be a real link between mental health and social media, but it's a complicated one, and not as dramatic or frightening as some might suggest. But it also reveals the limitations of the research into screens and mental health, and what we need to do to get better information.

Before we talk about what it found, though, it's worth explaining why it's so difficult to do good scientific work in this area in the first place.

Screens are not one thing

'"Social media" and "screen time" are pretty useless terms,' says Pete Etchells, a professor of psychology at Bath Spa University who is writing a book about our relationship with screens and technology. 'They cover a whole variety of things.'

His point is that 'screen time' isn't a simple thing. It would include Skyping family members, or playing Mario Kart with friends over the internet, or watching Match of the Day, or watching hardcore porn. These things are not like each other. And 'social media' isn't much better. Me doomscrolling through Twitter is not the same as a teenager making TikTok memes or a 65-year-old posting in a neighbourhood Facebook group.

More than that, mental health isn't a simple thing, either. Are we talking about 'psychological wellbeing', which is something like how happy or sad you are feeling, or how satisfied with your life, as reported on a questionnaire? Or are we talking about diagnoses of clinical mental health disorders, like depression and anxiety? Those are very different things, and are measured differently.

'If you look at 100 different papers in the area,' says Etchells, 'you'll find people talking about 100 different things.' For scientists in the field, he says, it's 'panic-inducing' to realise 'the vast scope of what we're trying to do. You ask a seemingly simple question: "there's this technology out there, how's it affecting our mental health?" But it's all a big mess.'

And it's very hard to show what is causing what. Most studies on these topics just look at a snapshot: thousands of people answer a questionnaire, which asks them questions about their social media use and their mental health: how satisfied are you with your life, with your appearance, and so on. And then they look for correlations: do people who use more social media tend also to report being less happy?

But if they do, what does that mean? If someone is using social media a lot, and they're also unhappy, is social media making them unhappy or – equally plausibly, on the face of it – are they using more social media because they're unhappy? Most people have surely had the experience of staring at their phone because they're not in the mood to be sociable.

And to complicate the matter even further, people's memories aren't very reliable. A 2019 study found that if you ask people how much they look at their phone, and at the same time use an app to record how much they actually look at it, the two numbers aren't very strongly linked. Self-reported data isn't useless, but it needs to be treated with caution.

That's why a lot of scientists, like Etchells, are very wary of much of the existing research. Despite some eye-catching findings, the studies are often not reliable, and more careful work frequently finds much more ambiguous results. Famously, one 2019 study found that the correlation between social media use and wellbeing was only about as strong as the correlation between regularly eating potatoes and wellbeing.

Ages of wonder

The new study did two interesting things. It looked at a wide range of ages, tracking the effect of social media across adolescence and in fact most of the human lifespan, and it considered whether social media use came first and changes in wellbeing followed them, or the other way around.

First, it looked at survey data from 72,000 people across the UK, from age 10 to 80. It asked people how much they used social media, and how they rated their satisfaction with life. But because it had such a huge sample size, it was able to break it down into age groups – you could see how 10-year-olds responded, and 11-year-olds, all the way up to 21-year-olds, and then broader categories for older age groups. It found that for most of the population, there's a 'Goldilocks effect': that is, people who use lots of social media tend to be more unhappy; people who never use it or who use it very little tend to be more unhappy; people who use a moderate amount tend to be the happiest. (If it seems surprising that young people who never use social media are less happy, imagine if you'd been cut off from a major means of communicating with your friends as a teenager.)

But that's not true for everyone. For young teenage girls, aged 13 and 14, and to a lesser extent for 15-year-olds of both sexes, there's a more straightforward relationship: on average, the more they use, the less happy they are.

This is important. 'Adolescents' aren't a monolithic block. A 12-year-old boy is a very different animal from a 19-year-old young woman, for instance. If there are times when social media can have a more profound effect, it's important to know.

Andrew Przybylski, a professor of psychology at the Oxford Internet Institute and one of the authors of the study, speculated that it might represent the onset of puberty: girls tend to go through puberty somewhat earlier than boys.

Cause and effect

The second part of the study tried to give an insight into what was causing what. As we discussed, it's easy to imagine that unhappier people spend more time on social media, rather than that social media is driving unhappiness.

So what the researchers did was look at young people's social media use and life satisfaction at one time, and then again a year later. The idea was that, usually, causes have to come before effects. If we saw that social media use went up only after life satisfaction went down, then that would suggest that social media couldn't be making people unhappy.

And that is, in fact, exactly what they found – most of the time. Young people who were unhappy one year tended to use social media more the next year. But at ages 11 to 13 for girls, 14 and 15 for boys, the relationship works both ways. Unhappier adolescents of those ages do use more social media, but those who use more social media seem to become less happy, as well.

That's also true for both sexes at age 19. Dr Amy Orben, a psychologist at Cambridge University's MRC Cognition and Brain Sciences Unit and the lead author on the study, suggests that this later age could be because of life changes, such as leaving school.

How much to worry?

These effects are small. Even at its strongest, the relationship between social media use one year and life satisfaction the next only explains about 4 per cent of the difference between people's scores on wellbeing questionnaires. And for most ages, social media use doesn't seem to affect life satisfaction at all, rather it's the other way around.

'This doesn't constitute advice to parents that their children should abstain from social media,' says Przybylski. 'It's clear from the data that abstinence isn't necessarily great, either.' That makes sense: if most children are communicating with their peers through social media, then cutting them off from social media means cutting off a lot of communication with their peers.

The fact that the results are small doesn't mean there's nothing to worry about – for one thing, we're talking about averages. 'We're stuck in this tyranny of averages,' says Orben.

'There's such massive individual variation.' Even if the average adolescent isn't harmed, people's personal experience might be that social media is really harmful for them or their child: there have been plenty of individual horror stories.

'If someone says that social media is really hurting – or benefiting – them in some way,' Orben says, 'I won't smack my study on the table and say no.' And more than that,

mental health is a complex and multifaceted thing, and perhaps small differences can have larger outcomes later on.

But for now, she says, 'it would be wrong to say more than that social media probably plays a tiny role among many factors.'

What happens next?

All the scientists I spoke to agree that we've reached the limits of what we can find out by looking for correlations between self-reported social media use and mental health. Przybylski in particular is trying to encourage social media companies like Facebook to share anonymised user data so that we can see more precisely what's going on. Orben says that one of her PhD students is working on links between clinical depression and social media, rather than life satisfaction.

For now, there is a lot of noise and confusion and concern, but still not a huge amount of solid data behind it. It's not entirely clear that there is a major epidemic of mental health issues in the UK – it may well be that people are simply more willing to talk about them and seek help for them, which would show up in the statistics as an increase. But if there is, it's not – at the moment – clear that social media is causing it.

'I'm talking as a university lecturer rather than as a psychologist,' says Etchells. 'But I have conversations with students about mental health. Lots of students are struggling with their mental health because of their finances, or because they're struggling with coursework, or because they can't access support services. Screens just don't come into it.

'Social media is an easy thing to point to, and we've all seen stories of when it's gone wrong, but life just isn't that simple.'

30 March 2022

The above information is reprinted with kind permission from *iNews*.
© 2022 Associated Newspapers Limited.

www.inews.co.uk

Children and parents: media use and attitudes report 2022

An Extract

Media use by age: a snapshot

3-4

17% have their own mobile phone

To go online: 39% use a mobile phone, 78% use a tablet and 10% use a laptop

89% use video sharing platfomrs
32% use live streaming apps/sites
50% use messaging sites/apps
21% use social media and 24% have their own social media profile
18% play games online
81% watch TV or films on any type of device other than a TV set (85% on a TV set)
47% watch live TV vs 72% who watch SVoD*

5-7

28% have their own mobile phone

To go online: 50% use a mobile phone, 83% use a tablet and 27% use a laptop

93% use video sharing platfomrs
39% use live streaming apps/sites
59% use messaging sites/apps
33% use social media and 33% have their own social media profile
38% play games online
74% watch TV or films on any type of device other than a TV set (88% on a TV set)
48% watch live TV vs 77% who watch SVoD*

8-11

60% have their own mobile phone

To go online: **71%** use a mobile phone, **79%** use a tablet and **55%** use a laptop

95% use video sharing platfomrs
54% use live streaming apps/sites
84% use messaging sites/apps
64% use social media and **60%** have their own social media profile
69% play games online
79% watch TV or films on any type of device other than a TV set (**90%** on a TV set)
51% watch live TV vs **76%** who watch SVoD*
32% have seen something worrying or nasty online 📶
32% were able to correctly identify sponsored search results 🔍

12-15

97% have their own mobile phone

To go online: **94%** use a mobile phone, **54%** use a tablet and **63%** use a laptop

98% use video sharing platfomrs
73% use live streaming apps/sites
97% use messaging sites/apps
91% use social media and **89%** have their own social media profile
76% play games online
87% watch TV or films on any type of device other than a TV set (**84%** on a TV set)
44% watch live TV vs **82%** who watch SVoD*
37% have seen something worrying or nasty online 📶
11% picked only reliable indicators that a social media post was genuine;📶 **83%** picked at least one unreliable indicator
64% were able to correctly spot a fake profile 📶
38% were able to correctly identify sponsored search results 🔍
39% were able to correctly identify sponsored content posted by an influencer 📶

16-17

100% have their own mobile phone

To go online: **98%** use a mobile phone, **50%** use a tablet and **63%** use a laptop

98% use video sharing platfomrs
79% use live streaming apps/sites
99% use messaging sites/apps
97% use social media and **94%** have their own social media profile
73% play games online
85% watch TV or films on any type of device other than a TV set (**82%** on a TV set)
44% watch live TV vs **79%** who watch SVoD*
42% have seen something worrying or nasty online 📶
13% picked only reliable indicators that a social media post was genuine;📶 **81%** picked at least one unreliable indicator
65% were able to correctly spot a fake profile 📶
44% were able to correctly identify sponsored search results 🔍
48% were able to correctly identify sponsored content posted by an influencer 📶

* SVoD: Subscription video on-demand services such as Netflix, Amazon Prime and Disney+
📶 Among those who go online   🔍 Among search engine users

Source: Ofcom - Children and parents: media use and attitudes report 2022

Online attitudes

Parents' views towards the benefits of being online versus the risks for their child varied greatly by the type of online activity

Parents of 3-17s were more likely to be positive about their child's use of the internet to gather information than they were about other social and entertainment activities. Almost six in ten parents agreed that the benefits of using the internet to gather information (for example using search engines, Wikipedia or news websites) outweighed the risks (58%). This compares to just four in ten who agreed that benefits outweighed the risks in relation to gaming (38%), and three in ten who agreed the same in relation to social media, messaging and video sharing (28%). While there were no differences by age group for gaming, parents of 12-17-year-olds were significantly more likely than parents of younger children aged 3-11 to feel that the benefits outweighed the risks for both information gathering and social media, messaging and video sharing.

Children were broadly positive about the benefits of being online but also recognised the negative sides

Six in ten children aged 8-17 who used social media or any messaging/ voice/ video calling apps/ sites felt that these types of platforms made them feel happy (59%) or closer to their friends (61%) all or most of the time. Girls were more likely than boys to agree with both statements, while boys were more likely to say they felt this only sometimes for both. Girls aged 12-17 were also more likely to use this form of media to send supportive messages to their friends if they were having a hard time (75% compared to 47% of boys this age). This feeling of closeness to their friends extended beyond their use of social media and messaging. Almost two-thirds of children aged 12-17 (64%) said that being online helped them to build and maintain friendships – again, more likely among girls than boys. But children are also aware of the negative aspects of using these platforms.

Eight in ten children aged 8-17 (78%) said they had felt, at some point, that people could be mean or unkind to each other on them. As with the positive side of social media, girls were more likely to say this than boys (81% vs 75%). Nine in ten 8-17-year-olds (89%) said they had ever felt pressure to be popular on these platforms, with no difference by gender.

Understanding the online space

'Critical understanding' is a core component of media literacy; it enables children to understand, question, and manage their media environment. This is important if they are to get the benefits that the internet and other media can offer while avoiding potential risks or harms. .

Gathering and checking information

One in ten children aged 8-17 think that everything they see on social media is true, while a majority think that only some of it is true

The internet can be a useful source of reliable, accurate information from a range of trustworthy sources, and going online can have a positive effect on everyone's learning, particularly among children. However, some information online is neither trustworthy nor reliable, and a media-literate child needs the skills which allow them to try to gather evidence and assess the validity of what they see. Part of this involves approaching information online with a degree of healthy scepticism.

Overall, our research suggested that most children are finding this balance. The majority of 8-17s who use social media thought that only some of what they see on social media is true (63%). However, one in ten believed that everything they see on social media is true (12%).

Children were also sceptical about news apps and sites, although a fifth believed that all they see on these is true

There was relatively little consensus about the extent of the truth and reliability of information on news apps and sites.

Parents' agreement that the benefits outweigh the risks of a child...

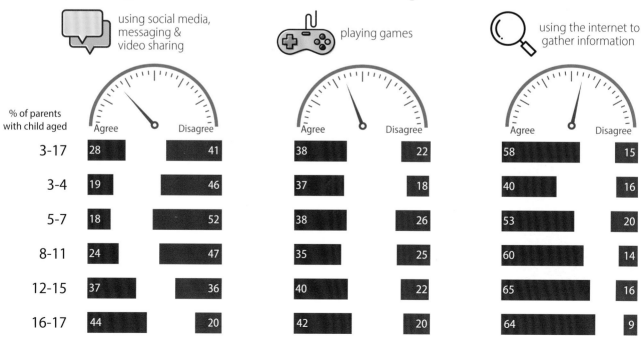

Source: Children and parents: media use and attitudes report 2022

A fifth of 8-17s who use news apps and sites (19%) believed that all the information on these was true, compared to more than two-fifths (44%) who thought that most was true and 31% believing that only some of it was true. The likelihood of selecting the 'all' option decreased with age.

Children were more trusting of apps and sites used for school and homework

A third of children aged 8-17 who use apps and sites for school or homework believed that everything they saw on these apps or sites was true – higher than the proportion who thought this of social media or news platforms (around a fifth for each). However, mirroring their views of news platforms, 40% thought that most of what they saw on school and homework apps and sites was true, while a quarter (24%) thought that just some of it was true.

Most children think about the trustworthiness of the information they encounter when they are using apps and sites they have never used before

A key skill in assessing the accuracy and reliability of online information is knowing when and how to use 'checking behaviours'; that is, behaviours that assess the accuracy and reliability of online sources and the information they provide. It is important to note, however, that checking behaviours do not always guarantee good outcomes. Reliance on aesthetic indicators like the look of a website, for example, could lead to false assessments of reliability. This is illustrated in practice by how the children responded to our misinformation scenario (see below).

The majority of children aged 12-17 (92%) who use apps and sites they have not used before in a typical week said they think about whether they can trust the truth and accuracy of information on these apps and sites. This figure was consistent across age and gender.

Children's checking behaviour often relied on aesthetic indicators or the overall impression of the platform

The most common checking behaviours employed by children aged 12-17 when using apps or sites they had not used before were: checking the general look of the website (45%), seeing if it was a company they had heard of (44%), and asking others if they had used the app or site before (42%).

Almost four in ten of these children checked information across multiple websites or checked how up-to-date the information on the site was (39% and 37% respectively). Checking behaviours can help a child to reach a more informed and rounded view of the site's trustworthiness and accuracy, either by assessing the information itself or by critically assessing the reliability of the source. They are not, however, a watertight way of guaranteeing that information is accurate. The most effective way of assessing the trustworthiness of a source would combine a variety of methods rather than relying on any particular one.

Assessing what is real and what is fake online

Three-quarters of children aged 12-17 claimed to be confident in their ability to judge what is real and what is fake online

Confidence does not just follow from good media literacy skills but intersects with it in a way which can either bolster or undermine good critical understanding. A child whose confidence is not matched by ability in practice may be more likely to make mistakes which could lead to harm. Conversely, a child who has good critical understanding skills but is not confident in them may not trust their own good judgement, which could lead them to feel unsure or unsafe in an online environment. More than seven in ten children aged 12-15 (72%) said that they were confident in judging what is real or fake online, compared to one in ten (12%) who said they were not. The older age group (16-17s) were more likely to be confident than 12-15s (78%), with boys aged 16-17 most confident of all (82%).

But more than eight in ten children aged 12-17 chose unreliable identifiers of information on a social media post

The importance of critical skills in assessing information, and identifying possible misinformation, has been made starkly clear during the Covid-19 pandemic. Our News Consumption Survey found that two-fifths of 12-15s said they had seen a deliberately untrue or misleading news story online in the past 12 months, but still more may be encountering misinformation without recognising it. Half of 12-15s who were surveyed said that they found it difficult to tell whether news on social media was accurate or not.

In 2021, we introduced online scenario questions in our media literacy surveys of children aged 12-17. One such

Children's assessment of whether info on an app/site is accurate and true

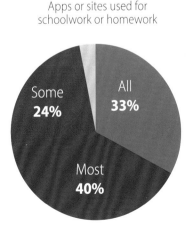

Apps or sites used for schoolwork or homework

Some 24%
All 33%
Most 40%

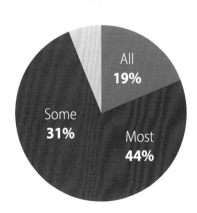

News apps or sites

All 19%
Some 31%
Most 44%

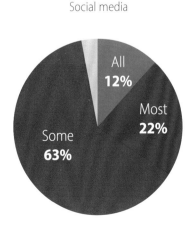

Social media

All 12%
Most 22%
Some 63%

Source: Children and parents: media use and attitudes report 2022

scenario was created from a genuine NHS Instagram post relating to Covid-19 vaccinations. Respondents were shown the post as it would appear to them on their phone screen and were then asked to pick out features or identifiers which suggested that the information on this post was accurate and reliable (our 'misinformation' scenario). The features which were classed as 'reliable' identifiers of authenticity are shown below. It is important to note that features which are marked as 'unreliable' are not always identifiers of a fake or misleading profile; for example, a genuine account may indeed have many followers. However, these features are not always identifiers of authenticity. A spam account, for example, could easily use a logo from a trusted organisation and could attract many followers, and sensational posts which include misleading information may attract many likes.

Just one in ten children aged 12-17 (11%) chose only the reliable identifiers from the misinformation scenario, with no differences by age. More than eight in ten (82%) chose at least one unreliable indicator.

In line with the prominence of checking the 'look' of a website, the most commonly chosen unreliable indicators of authenticity were aesthetic. The majority of children (70%) incorrectly thought that the logo shown in the mocked-up post suggested that the post was genuine, suggesting that well-designed fake apps and sites could be successful in misleading children, even if checking behaviour is in place.

The majority of 12-17s claimed to be confident in their ability to spot misinformation, but most were unable to do so in practice

We can plot reported confidence against performance in the misinformation scenario to give a picture of overall levels of critical understanding in relation to misinformation. Our data shows that three-quarters of children aged 12-17 (74%) had confidence in their ability to spot fake information; however, less than one in ten demonstrated both confidence and ability in this type of critical understanding.

When shown a fake social media profile, more than a fifth of 12-17s identified a fake profile as a genuine one

In addition to our misinformation scenario mentioned above, we asked 12-17s to take part in a scenario question involving a fake Instagram profile, and to judge whether they thought the profile was real or fake. They were then asked to pick out identifiers which influenced their decision using a 'heat map' technique. For example, they might choose the user's profile picture, the information in their 'bio', the number of followers or the username.

When presented with this image, the majority (64%) realised it was a fake profile. However, more than a fifth (22%) thought it was real, while 14% were unsure. There were no differences in these proportions between the two age groups, 12-15s and 13-17s. But boys were significantly more likely than girls to be unsure about whether the profile was real (17% vs 12%).

The most frequently chosen *unreliable identifiers* on this fake profile were the profile picture and the posted photos: more than a quarter of the children who said that they thought the profile was real identified these as evidence of this. Again, this suggests an over-reliance on aesthetic indicators which can be easily faked to boost perceptions that a profile is genuine. One in ten of this group (11%) selected the number of followers, which is slightly more difficult to fake but is still not a reliable indicator of authenticity (particularly as followers may sometimes be 'bought', despite platform guidelines preventing this).

Among those who thought the profile was fake, the majority felt this because of the details in the bio (75%), and just under half thought it because of the link in the description (45%).

In contrast to those who thought the profile was real, those who did not believe this were more sceptical of the number of followers on the post; a third of them felt that this was evidence of a fake profile.

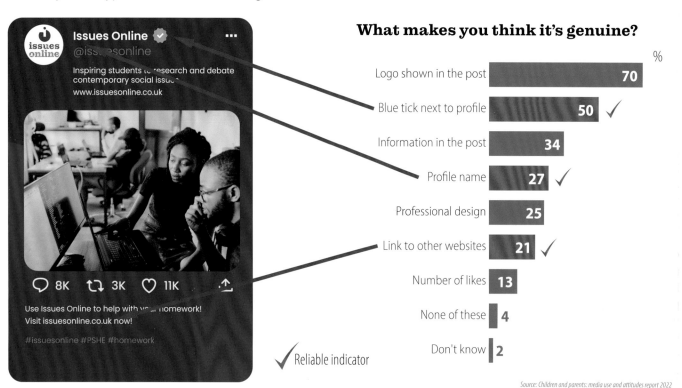

What makes you think it's genuine?

%

Logo shown in the post	70
Blue tick next to profile	50 ✓
Information in the post	34
Profile name	27 ✓
Professional design	25
Link to other websites	21 ✓
Number of likes	13
None of these	4
Don't know	2

✓ Reliable indicator

Source: Children and parents: media use and attitudes report 2022

Children aged 12-17 were much more likely to have confidence and ability in recognising a fake social media profile than in a misinformation post

Plotting children's confidence in spotting what is real and fake against their performance in the fake profile scenario, we see in the above graphic that children performed better in spotting a fake profile than they did in assessing indicators of authenticity in the misinformation scenario. Almost half the children were both confident and able in the fake profile scenario, compared to just over a quarter who were confident but *not* able.

Harmful or risky experiences

Negative experiences among children

Four in ten users aged 8-17 felt that people are mean to one another on social media and messaging services

Our research showed that children are aware of the potentially negative aspects and impacts of being online, and this increased with age. Four in ten children aged 8-17 (39%) who use social media, or any messaging apps and sites, agreed that people are mean or unkind to each other on these platforms either most (23%) or all (16%) of the time.

An even higher percentage of children using these services agreed that there is pressure to be popular online: nine in ten (89%) felt this at least sometimes, and one in ten (11%) believed that there was this pressure all the time.

More than a third of children aged 8-17 had encountered worrying or nasty content online, and some may inadvertently be sharing it further

Over a third of children aged 8-17 (36%) said they had seen something 'worrying or nasty' online in the past 12 months. The youngest age group (8-11s) was significantly less likely (32%) than 16-17s (42%) to say that they had seen something that worried them.

In some instances, children can contribute to the potential harm to other users through their actions online. This may be done with a degree of intentionality, for example through peer-on-peer cyberbullying or sharing 'edgy' humorous content which may offend others, or it could be done unintentionally.

A child with limited media literacy skills may, for example, share a piece of misinformation which they have mistakenly viewed as reliable. In addition to this, children may unwittingly contribute to the amplification of content (that is, its recommendation to other users through algorithms) by sharing or commenting on a piece of content. Even when this is done with the intention of denouncing or correcting the content, it contributes to the likelihood of that content being shown to others.

Our News Consumption Survey found that 15% of 12-15s said they would leave a comment on a piece of misinformation identifying it as 'fake news', and 14% would share it with people to tell them it was not true. By doing this, children may unwittingly be spreading this potentially harmful content further.

Two participants in our Children's Media Lives study also talked about sharing content which could be harmful. They recognised that the content could be offensive but shared it because they thought it was funny. Nathan (15) regularly shared offensive content, or content involving violence, on his Instagram. Sean (12) had shared a meme that included offensive content about people with learning disabilities.

When asked about this content, neither Nathan nor Sean felt that it was particularly offensive or had thought about why some of it might be upsetting to others. Nathan saw dark humour as part of his online personality and said that he was known among his group of friends for making 'out there' jokes.

Among children aged 8-17 who have experienced bullying, more than eight in ten experienced it through a communications device such as a phone or laptop

Two-thirds of parents of 3-17-year-olds said that they were worried about their child being bullied online. Concern about online bullying was highest among parents of 8-11s (76%) and 12-15s (71%).

Four in ten children aged 8-17 (39%) said that they had experienced some sort of bullying, whether online or offline. Among these, being bullied through communications technology was more prevalent than in person or face-to-face (84% vs 61%). Of those bullied via technology, the most common way was via text or messaging apps (56%), followed by 43% who said it had happened over social media.

For the youngest age group (8-11s) and the oldest (16-17s), being bullied face-to-face was the most likely method. However, for 12-15s it was via text or messaging apps (71% compared to 61% bullied face-to-face in this age group).

Likelihood of telling someone

More than nine in ten children aged 8-17 said they would tell someone if they encountered something upsetting online, especially 8-11s

The vast majority of children said that they would tell someone if they saw something worrying or nasty online: 93% said they would do this at least sometimes, and six in ten (59%) said they would always tell someone. The proportion of children saying that they would tell someone decreased with age, from 96% of 8-11s and 92% of 12-15s to 86% of 16-17s. Children aged 8-11 were also more likely to say they would always tell someone (71%) than either 12-15s (54%) or 16-17s (44%).

Girls were significantly more likely than boys to say that they would always tell someone about something worrying or nasty that they had seen (62% vs 56%). Boys were three times more likely than girls to be unsure, or to say they didn't know if they would tell anyone (6% vs 2%).

All age groups were most likely to say they would tell a parent (85% of 8-17s) – highest among children aged 8-11 (92%). Three in ten would tell a friend, and a quarter would tell a teacher. Only 8% of children and young people said they would tell the app/site where they saw the worrying content, rising to 15% among 16-17s. The oldest children were much more likely than any other age group to say they would tell a friend (43% compared to 20% of 8-11s and 36% of 12-15s).

Methods of bullying

% of those who have been bullied

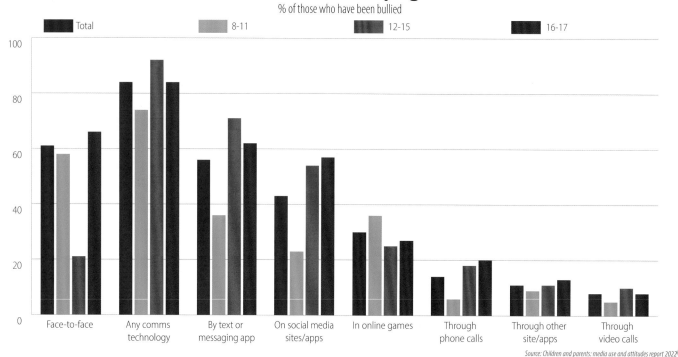

Total   8-11   12-15   16-17

Source: Children and parents: media use and attitudes report 2022

A fifth of parents of 3-17s said their child had told them about something upsetting they had seen online

In 2021, a fifth of parents of 3-17s said their child had told them about something they had seen online that had scared or upset them in the past 12 months, with little difference across the age groups. The youngest children (aged 3-4) were less likely than all older children to have told their parent about something scary or upsetting (12%), but among the older age groups the percentages were between 20% and 23%.

Among those whose child had told them, the most common action was to talk with their child about their experience (89%). Other actions taken were advising their child to stop using the app or site (59%) or advising them to block the people/ content concerned (55%). Three in ten (31%) reported the content to the platform where their child had seen it, a quarter set up filters or parental controls, and just under a quarter (23%) sought advice on how to handle the situation from other sources.

Preventative and safety measures

Good critical understanding among adults has the potential to help children avoid harms online. One of the ways in which adults, including parents and carers, can help children build their critical understanding is by talking to them about online safety, making them aware of safer ways to use the internet, and by using technical controls and settings within services and devices.

Measures among children

Nine in ten children have been spoken to about online safety, most likely by a parent or teacher

Nine in ten children aged 8-17 who go online have had someone speak to them about how to use the internet safely; 8-11s are the most likely group to have had this (94%).

These children were most likely to say they had been spoken to about internet safety by a parent (89%), followed by a teacher at school (69%). Children aged 8-11 were the most likely to say they had been spoken to about internet safety by a teacher.

Nearly all children knew how to carry out at least one safety-promoting behaviour online, and more than eight in ten had put their knowledge into practice

Nearly all children aged 12-17 were aware of at least one safety-promoting behaviour (94%). And a lower, but still substantial, proportion of children (84%) said they had carried out or used at least one.

Blocking people on social media was the safety-promoting behaviour with both the highest awareness (81%) and the highest use (66%) – both more likely among 16-17-year-olds than 12-15s. While girls were as likely to be aware of this behaviour as boys, they were more likely to use it in practice (70% vs 62%).

Two-thirds of 12-17s were aware of how to block people within online games (65%), with boys being more likely than girls to be both aware (74% vs 56% of girls) and to use (59% vs 36% of girls) this feature.

Girls were also more likely than boys to be aware of and to use settings in social media so that fewer people could see their profile (56% of girls were aware, vs 49% of boys, and 33% of girls do this, vs 27% of boys). Older children (16-17) were more likely to do this than the 12-15s, with 53% of 12-17s overall being aware of this feature and 30% using it.

Awareness of online reporting or flagging functions was low among children, and only a minority had actually used them

A third of 12-17s said that they knew how to use a reporting or flagging function (32%), but only 14% said they had used any of them. Unlike many other behaviours, features and technologies, neither use nor awareness of the reporting or flagging function varied with age or by gender.

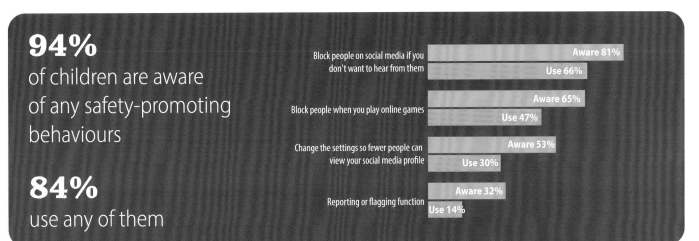

94%
of children are aware
of any safety-promoting
behaviours

84%
use any of them

Block people on social media if you don't want to hear from them — Aware 81% / Use 66%
Block people when you play online games — Aware 65% / Use 47%
Change the settings so fewer people can view your social media profile — Aware 53% / Use 30%
Reporting or flagging function — Aware 32% / Use 14%

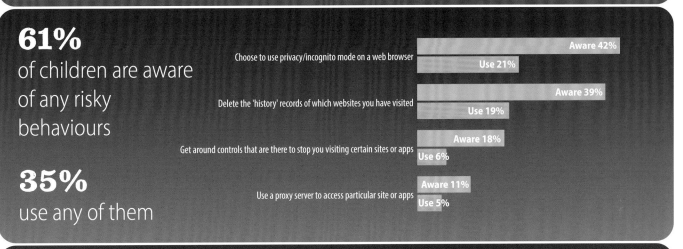

61%
of children are aware
of any risky
behaviours

35%
use any of them

Choose to use privacy/incognito mode on a web browser — Aware 42% / Use 21%
Delete the 'history' records of which websites you have visited — Aware 39% / Use 19%
Get around controls that are there to stop you visiting certain sites or apps — Aware 18% / Use 6%
Use a proxy server to access particular site or apps — Aware 11% / Use 5%

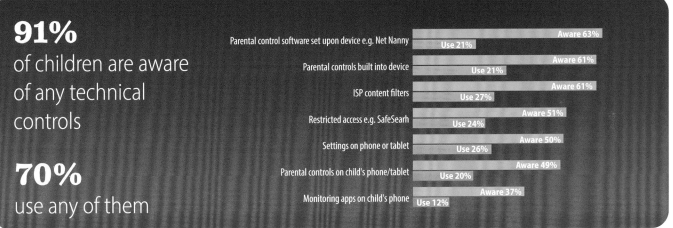

91%
of children are aware
of any technical
controls

70%
use any of them

Parental control software set upon device e.g. Net Nanny — Aware 63% / Use 21%
Parental controls built into device — Aware 61% / Use 21%
ISP content filters — Aware 61% / Use 27%
Restricted access e.g. SafeSearh — Aware 51% / Use 24%
Settings on phone or tablet — Aware 50% / Use 26%
Parental controls on child's phone/tablet — Aware 49% / Use 20%
Monitoring apps on child's phone — Aware 37% / Use 12%

Source: Children and parents: media use and attitudes report 2022

Some privacy-promoting measures may have the effect of making children less safe online

In addition to features, behaviours and technologies which promote online safety, many platforms, device manufacturers and software companies offer options to promote privacy. While these have a valid and potentially positive role in the online lives of adults, when they are used by children, online safety may be compromised. For example, if a child uses private or 'incognito' browsing or deletes their browsing history, a parent may not be able to check on their online use and identify or report instances of potentially harmful content or behaviour.

When asked which measures they used to protect themselves online, more than a third of children aged 12-17 (35%) reported using measures which might in fact have put them more at risk, because they could enable them to come across potentially harmful content. This included a fifth who had surfed in incognito mode (21%), had deleted their browsing history (19%), and one in twenty who had circumvented parental controls put in place to stop them visiting certain apps and sites (6%), or used a proxy server to access particular apps and sites (5%).

Four in ten children aged 16-17 (42%) reported that they had carried out one or more of these behaviours – higher than the proportion of 12-15s (31%). This included a quarter of 16-17s who had surfed using privacy mode (25%) or who had deleted their internet history (24%).

30 March 2022

The above information is reprinted with kind permission from Ofcom.
© 2022 Ofcom

www.ofcom.org.uk

YouTube comments bombarded with porn and scam links targeting channels with millions of young fans

Child safety charities have urged the video giant to do more to protect young users from harmful material.

By Tom Saunders

Spam commenters are flooding popular YouTube channels with links containing suspected scams and directing young audiences towards pornographic websites.

An i investigation found comments sections on channels such as that of MrBeast – a YouTuber famous for viral stunts with more than 94 million subscribers – were bombarded with spam comments despite YouTube claiming to have addressed the problem in 2019.

Using an open-source spam detection algorithm, our investigation found that on a number of popular channels with millions of subscribers, spam comments made up around one in five comments.

i was able to find at least 20 different comments encouraging users to visit X-rated websites on a recent video on the YouTube channel of best-selling video game Fortnite.

A number of different accounts and messages were shared in the comments thread but most appeared to be directing gamers to the same explicit sites through X-rated accounts.

A mixture of posts is likely to have been used in a bid to avoid spam filters which can be alerted by repetitive posts.

Andy Burrows, NSPCC Head of Child Safety Online Policy, said: 'It is concerning that young YouTube users are being increasingly targeted and directed to potentially harmful pornographic sites and encouraged to click on links that falsely promise free online currency for games.

'YouTube should be taking steps to make sure children aren't being unwittingly directed to pornographic material, or lured into clicking such links.'

Other spam messages include scam attempts in which some fraudsters attempt to impersonate the accounts of popular YouTubers and encourage fans to click on links or enter bank details through supposed giveaways or competitions.

One account, with the name 'Telegram me????Mrbeast555', and featuring the same logo as the official MrBeast account, replied to at least 22 different comments with the same phrase: 'Congratulations you have just been selected hit me up to claim your price ???? ????..'.

The issue has already forced some YouTubers to alert their own subscribers.

Jeff Geerling, a Youtuber with 309,000 subscribers who makes videos where he builds and tests tech products, said in response to an online discussion about the wave of scams: 'At this point, every one of my videos is targeted, and usually in waves two or three times before the spammers give up.

'Sadly, there are at least 5-10 people *per week* who now email me asking if the scam is legit, and I have to tell them no, I would never choose you to win something then ask you to send me $100 to send it to you.'

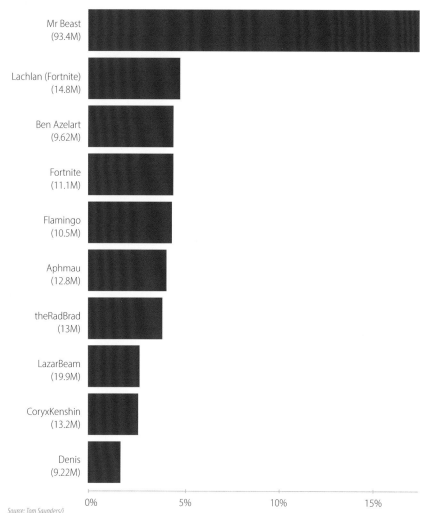

YouTube spam comments

Proportion of sampled comments detected as Spam by i's spam detector

- Mr Beast (93.4M)
- Lachlan (Fortnite) (14.8M)
- Ben Azelart (9.62M)
- Fortnite (11.1M)
- Flamingo (10.5M)
- Aphmau (12.8M)
- theRadBrad (13M)
- LazarBeam (19.9M)
- CoryxKenshin (13.2M)
- Denis (9.22M)

0%   5%   10%   15%

Source: Tom Saunders/i

YouTube spam comments

Number of times the most prolific Spam author commented on the same video

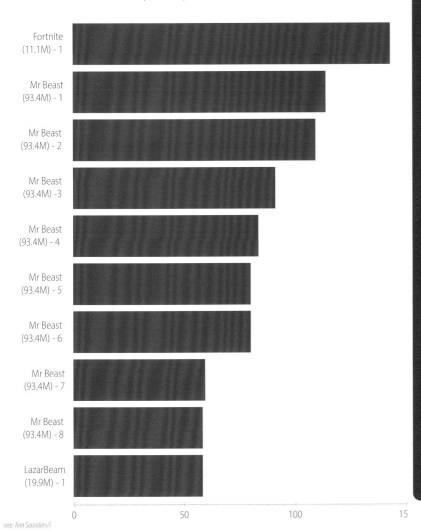

Fortnite (11.1M) - 1	
Mr Beast (93.4M) - 1	
Mr Beast (93.4M) - 2	
Mr Beast (93.4M) -3	
Mr Beast (93.4M) - 4	
Mr Beast (93.4M) - 5	
Mr Beast (93.4M) - 6	
Mr Beast (93.4M) - 7	
Mr Beast (93.4M) - 8	
LazarBeam (19.9M) - 1	

0   50   100   15

urce: Tom Saunders/i

Techniques used by YouTube spammers

Two broad categories of spam comments are present on these videos and both categories exist mainly thanks to changes YouTube has made to its comment sections over the years.

One form of spam comment tries to entice Youtube users off-site onto X-rated platforms. This is particularly problematic as many of the channels targeted are often those who have younger audiences.

While these spam comments are ostensibly being employed by various different actors, the method is largely the same and uses the fact that YouTube does not require authentic usernames, making it far easier to impersonate other users.

It's not clear whether these comments are made by automated bots or humans, but the high number of comments from individual accounts suggest that they could be from bots.

The other most prevalent category of spam is scammers who impersonate the channel's author by changing their name and profile picture to match. They then reply to comments claiming that they have won a prize and encourage the user to move onto an offsite platform.

Internet safety groups have warned children are particularly vulnerable to such scams where their fandom is preyed upon by opportunists.

Will Gardner, Childnet CEO and a director of the UK Safer Internet Centre, says: 'Remember that comments on YouTube and across social media platforms can come from anyone. Even "famous" people may not be who they say they are and anyone, even famous people, can say unreliable things. Regardless of their number of followers or if they have a verified account, it's still important to critically assess content associated with them.

'We advise young people to think critically to ensure they are navigating the internet safely and finding reliable information. Question what you see online, even if it looks official or promises something exciting; if something seems too good to be true, it probably isn't.'

Impersonation scams have regularly been seen on YouTube comment sections for several years.

YouTube previously claimed to have made changes to address the problem back in January 2019, stating in a tweet that they were 'in the process of implementing additional measures to prevent impersonation like this.'

YouTube currently does have capabilities for combatting Spam such as an automatic spam filter. However, it's unclear how much this does to combat spam on the platform.

Popular tech YouTuber Marques Brownlee shared a video earlier this month where he disclosed that despite using the filter he had 39 different accounts on his most recent video all impersonating him, commenting between one and 111 times on the same video.

Imran Ahmed, Chief Executive of the Center for Countering Digital Hate (CCDH), said: 'Google always has to be forced kicking and screaming to implement even the most basic safety tools.

'Big Tech thinks it is a law unto itself, but the era of self-regulation has been an unambiguous failure. It's time the government incentivised action by ensuring YouTube suffers penalties for turning a blind eye to fraud on their platform.'

A YouTube spokesperson said: 'Upon review, we have removed many of the flagged comments for violating our spam policies. In Q4 2021, we removed over 3.4 million channels, over 339,000 videos and over 950 million comments for violating our policies around spam, scams and deceptive practices.'

24 April 2022

The above information is reprinted with kind permission from *iNews*.
© 2022 Associated Newspapers Limited.

www.inews.co.uk

What is the metaverse – and what do I need to know?

Tech observers have been talking for some time about the 'metaverse'. The online and offline worlds have already begun to merge in many ways, with education, services and social life now available online.

The metaverse takes this to the next level, using radical new technologies, to make livable, virtual worlds.

But what actually is the metaverse? What does it mean for the future of tech and the internet? And how will it affect the younger generation who may experience it, eventually, as commonplace?

What is the metaverse?

The name 'metaverse' isn't actually that new: it first appeared in a dystopian 1992 novel, Snow Crash, by the sci-fi writer Neal Stephenson.

It's a term for a combination of virtual reality with other technologies that will allow us to have a deeper experience of the online world. The metaverse is a 3D environment in which we can interact, rather than seeing the internet simply on a screen.

Using virtual reality headsets or augmented reality glasses – at least initially – the metaverse promises the ability to live in imagined worlds in the same way we live in the physical world.

We'll be able to travel virtually to beautiful beaches, see our favourite bands no matter where they're playing, try on clothing, create avatars that have their own independent lives and love affairs – you name it. It's a concept that you may have seen explored in the 2018 Steven Speilberg movie *Ready Player One*.

The soaring popularity in cryptocurrencies and NFTs – non-fungible tokens, or unique digital objects – are also a part of the metaverse phenomenon. For someone not involved in this culture, it might be hard to understand how value can lie in things that are immaterial. But for enthusiasts of the metaverse, there is real value in virtual experiences and perceptions.

Why is the metaverse important?

The metaverse could bring the online and offline worlds closer together. This could be great; you might, for example, try on clothes or test drive a vehicle virtually and then buy them in reality. It could also offer pure escapism and entertainment.

It's difficult to predict exactly what it will be used for because, despite all the talk, the metaverse is still largely a dream – even within technology companies.

Which tech companies are exploring the metaverse?

Facebook most notably rebranded their holding company Meta – outlining their vision of the metaverse in a promotional video featuring numerous virtual environments.

Meta (i.e. Facebook) expects to spend billions of dollars and has announced its intention to hire 10,000 staff in Europe alone to work on its development. Meta is also developing new services to create a more coherent world, such as a cryptocurrency wallet called Novi and a communication tool called Workplace.

But they are not alone. Microsoft has also begun exploring the metaverse, partly as a way of making remote work easier following the Covid-19 pandemic. They've created a new service called Mesh that uses mixed-reality technologies, allowing people to work together virtually.

But perhaps the gaming industry is already well ahead of the game in embracing the metaverse – at least in a commercial sense. The gaming platform Roblox, for example, already connects users in online spaces, offering them tools to create and share their own games, or, as the company sometimes calls them, 'experiences'. Users can assemble their own avatars rather than being tied to pre-existing characters.

Earlier this year, a virtual Gucci bag sold on Roblox for more than $4,000. The bag can't be transferred out of Roblox, which gives some indication of how much people might be prepared to invest in how they are perceived in the metaverse.

What do we need to be aware of?

The effect on children

Many companies hope the metaverse will engage a younger audience which has been waning for companies like Meta. Lots of young people believe strongly in accessibility and community for all, something that the metaverse promises.

But unfortunately, we can't tell whether this will be how the metaverse actually plays out. In the meantime, there are some risks specific to children that are worth considering. Virtual reality technology is still new, and there hasn't been a huge amount of research into what effects it might have at such an early age.

Despite having lots of benefits, social media sites have already proven to be damaging for some children in terms of functionality, privacy and moderation. But the move into the metaverse could make bullying or insecurity feel even more immediate and upsetting.

Tech companies may also realise the pull of the metaverse for children and design services that could manipulate them into spending large sums of money with little gain.

Detachment and tech company power

One dystopian vision is that people will be deflected from real-world problems and, as a result, will be more vulnerable to being manipulated. While the planet heats up, and politicians and tech billionaires amass ever more power and money, people will be lulled into passivity by the virtual rewards of the metaverse.

The more immediate concern is that tech companies will use this more invasive technology to harvest even more data from users – not just about our behaviour, but about our hopes, dreams and imaginations. Tech companies are already being accused of modifying our behaviour: what will they be able to do with this even more intimate knowledge?

Limiting choice

Companies that use a metaverse model will have more power than ones that don't, simply because they incorporate more services. In some ways, this promises convenience. But it also raises the question of how much power we feel comfortable with tech companies having. The metaverse model could lead companies further towards being a kind of digital state. We discussed this on the Tech Shock podcast with Tracey Follows.

If a single company, or even a few companies, are allowed to dominate, in the end that will limit consumer choice and prevent new ideas and enterprises entering the market.

What happens next?

An increasing number of businesses are taking an interest in the metaverse. For all the talk, we still need to think carefully about how the metaverse will influence our external lives.

It's going to be important to keep children in the loop and listen to their thoughts on what a full blown virtual reality and services might mean. Try to ask them how they feel about the metaverse as a concept – are they excited, worried, or just curious?

The metaverse will enhance all aspects of life, and make whatever we have at the moment 'more'. Whilst that's great for our positive experiences, it might also make bad experiences much worse. What seems certain is that there will be much more talk about the metaverse – and much more controversy – before we fully understand what it is.

The above information is reprinted with kind permission from Parent Zone.
© 2022 Parent Zone

www.parentzone.org.uk

What is the 'metaverse'? The meaning behind Facebook's plans to build a VR world as it announces 10,000 jobs

Facebook is hiring 10,000 new workers in Europe to help make its metaverse dreams a (virtual) reality – but what does it all mean?

By Rhiannon Williams

While Silicon Valley is no stranger to jargon, 'metaverse' is one term that's becoming increasingly familiar.

Facebook, the highest-profile champion of the metaverse, has announced plans to hire 10,000 people in the European Union to build it. But what exactly is it?

What is the metaverse?

The origins of the metaverse stretch back to 1992, when American author Neal Stephenson coined the term in his seminal and highly influential sci-fi novel Snow Crash to describe what is essentially a virtual reality (VR)-based version of the internet.

The metaverse, according to Stephenson, is a sprawling multiplayer universe that participants traverse using digital avatars, similar to the ideas explored by fellow author William Gibson in 1982 short story Burning Chrome and 1984's Neuromancer – which went on to heavily influence 1999's The Matrix.

Ernest Cline expanded upon these fundamental tenets in his novel and later Hollywood film Ready Player One, in which the OASIS metaverse offers people a welcome virtual escape from the drudgery of their lives in the dystopian real world.

Inspired by the notion of this interconnected fictional vision, the likes of Facebook want to make the metaverse a (virtual) reality – 'a set of virtual spaces where you can create and explore with other people who aren't in the same physical space as you', complete with a $50 million investment pledge last month.

Visitors to these virtual spaces will be able to work, play, learn, shop, create and hang out with friends, among other activities, it explains, adding that it's 'not necessarily about spending more time online — it's about making the time you do spend online more meaningful'.

The social network continues its definition of the metaverse in typically buzzword-heavy terms – 'a new phase of interconnected virtual experiences using technologies like virtual and augmented reality' – at the heart of which is 'the idea that by creating a greater sense of 'virtual presence', interacting online can become much closer to the experience of interacting in person', according to its vice president of global affairs Nick Clegg.

Like the internet, the metaverse will not be built, owned or operated by one company alone, will lessen our reliance of physical devices to access virtual spaces and is likely to be under construction for another 10 to 15 years, the company has projected.

What about the jobs?

Facebook has committed to hiring 10,000 highly specialised engineers based in the EU over the next five years to build the computing platform, which the company has called a vote of confidence in the strength of the European tech industry and the potential of European tech talent more widely.

It added it was looking forward to working with European governments to hire the right people in the right markets.

'Beyond emerging tech talent, the EU also has an important role to play in shaping the new rules of the internet,' Mr Clegg added.

'European policymakers are leading the way in helping to embed European values like free expression, privacy, transparency and the rights of individuals into the day-to-day workings of the internet.

'Facebook shares these values and we have taken considerable action over the years to uphold them.'

18 October 2021

The above information is reprinted with kind permission from *iNews*.
© 2022 Associated Newspapers Limited.

www.inews.co.uk

Metaverse: a passing trend or an internet revolution?

A young person shares his thoughts on what the future of the Metaverse looks like.

By Abdul Moiz

I think the Metaverse is going to be a complete fad and not something that will become an integral part of our everyday lives. Truth be told, we are already in a Metaverse; how? Metaverse is a concept where real life and digital life are intermingled together. Our "Metaverse" journey began when PCs and smartphones got popular, which helped us with productivity and also created our digital presence/life online.

Mark Zuckerberg is creating hype for a product (Metaverse) that is slated to launch by 2025 — this sounds a bit like Theranos, doesn't it?

Metaverse is doomed to fail, and here's how!

Metaverse is a cash cow

With the announcement of Metaverse, Mark Zuckerberg managed to create a buzz that is helping him stay afloat amid many accusations regarding privacy and monopoly.

Many other tech giants are also working on a similar platform, such as Microsoft, Nike, Epic Games, Tencent, Snapchat, and more, and there is nothing special about Meta's Metaverse.

Amongst a few features that were mentioned in the event, Mark Zuckerberg, in his announcement, said how remote working will be possible through Metaverse's digital workspace and how every user will choose their character's looks and outfit.

Why is this a breakthrough feature? Video calls help us interact on a more personal and intimate level. And video calls are the best alternative for someone who cannot meet their co-workers or their loved ones in person.

Metaverse has not even launched yet, but digital lands for Metaverse are being sold already! In fact, many companies are heavily investing in setting up the digital world of their brand for Metaverse, which yet to be released.

This looks like a modern-day dot-com bubble that will leave the tech community, the investors, and the whole world in shock when it falls.

Everybody says metaverse is the next big thing

Everyone said registering the domain with dot-com is a solid path to success, but we know what happened.

Everyone said the Internet is just a fad, and we know what happened. The point is the Internet is a breakthrough innovation, and the dot-com isn't!

Metaverse will be another platform to play games, and host digital parties, and events. But not the way we are imagining. The hype train is on because it's a new product in the technological space, and everyone is hoping it to be a groundbreaking product. But the chances are very slim for it to become successful.

Metaverse also has lots of infrastructure challenges that will be hard to overcome.

Metaverse and the bandwidth

Metaverse has lots of challenges ahead, and this is why Mark Zuckerberg is working relentlessly to eliminate the challenges, but is it possible?

A fast and reliable internet connection is still a dream of many. Metaverse requires a fast internet connection, with low latency, for a seamless and real-time interaction in the Metaverse.

If the internet connection is unstable or has high latency, the experience will be the same as our video chat/conference getting disconnected or paused for a few seconds — infuriating!

There is hope

The way I see it, Metaverse has very little scope to turn out to become what it has been claiming to become — the "Next big thing." Metaverse can be an excellent device for gaming and media consumption but nothing more than that.

It is yet to be seen how this device is going to turn out in the future. But, one thing is for sure the future is not going to be like Ready Player One.

24 March 2022

The above information is reprinted with kind permission from Youth Zone.
© 2022 Youth Zone

www.voicebox.site

Protecting children in the metaverse: it's easy to blame big tech, but we all have a role to play

An article from *The Conversation*.   THE CONVERSATION

By Andy Phippen, Professor of IT Ethics and Digital Rights, Bournemouth University

I n a recent BBC news investigation, a reporter posing as a 13-year-old girl in a virtual reality (VR) app was exposed to sexual content, racist insults and a rape threat. The app in question, VRChat, is an interactive platform where users can create 'rooms' within which people interact (in the form of avatars). The reporter saw avatars simulating sex, and was propositioned by numerous men.

The results of this investigation have led to warnings from child safety charities including the National Society for the Prevention of Cruelty to Children (NSPCC) about the dangers children face in the metaverse. The metaverse refers to a network of VR worlds which Meta (formerly Facebook) has positioned as a future version of the internet, eventually allowing us to engage across education, work and social contexts.

The NSPCC appears to put the blame and the responsibility on technology companies, arguing they need to do more to safeguard children's safety in these online spaces. While I agree platforms could be doing more, they can't tackle this problem alone.

Reading about the BBC investigation, I felt a sense of déjà vu. I was surprised that anyone working in online safeguarding would be – to use the NSPCC's words – 'shocked' by the reporter's experiences. Ten years ago, well before we'd heard the word 'metaverse', similar stories emerged around platforms including Club Penguin and Habbo Hotel.

These avatar-based platforms, where users interact in virtual spaces via a text-based chat function, were actually designed for children. In both cases adults posing as children as a means to investigate were exposed to sexually explicit interactions.

The demands that companies do more to prevent these incidents have been around for a long time. We are locked in a cycle of new technology, emerging risks and moral panic. Yet nothing changes.

It's a tricky area

We've seen demands for companies to put age verification measures in place to prevent young people accessing inappropriate services. This has included proposals for social platforms to require verification that the user is aged 13 or above, or for pornography websites to require proof that the user is over 18.

If age verification was easy, it would have been widely adopted by now. If anyone can think of a way that all 13-year-olds can prove their age online reliably, without data privacy concerns, and in a way that's easy for platforms to implement, there are many tech companies that would like to talk to them.

In terms of policing the communication that occurs on these platforms, similarly, this won't be achieved through an algorithm. Artificial intelligence is nowhere near clever enough to intercept real-time audio streams and determine, with accuracy, whether someone is being offensive. And while there might be some scope for human moderation, monitoring of all real-time online spaces would be impossibly resource-intensive.

The reality is that platforms already provide a lot of tools to tackle harassment and abuse. The trouble is few people are aware of them, believe they will work, or want to use them. VRChat, for example, provides tools for blocking abusive users, and the means to report them, which might ultimately result in the user having their account removed.

We cannot all sit back and shout, 'my child has been upset by something online, who is going to stop this from happening?'. We need to shift our focus from the notion of 'evil big tech', which really isn't helpful, to looking at the role other stakeholders could play too.

If parents are going to buy their children VR headsets, they need to have a look at safety features. It's often possible to monitor activity by having the young person cast what is on their headset onto the family TV or another screen. Parents could also check out the apps and games young people are interacting with prior to allowing their children to use them.

What young people think

I've spent the last two decades researching online safeguarding – discussing concerns around online harms with young people, and working with a variety of stakeholders on how we might better help young people. I rarely hear demands that the government needs to bring big tech companies to heel from young people themselves.

They do, however, regularly call for better education and support from adults in tackling the potential online harms they might face. For example, young people tell us they want discussion in the classroom with informed teachers who can manage the debates that arise, and to whom they can ask questions without being told 'don't ask questions like that'.

However, without national coordination, I can sympathise with any teacher not wishing to risk complaint from, for example, outraged parents, as a result of holding a discussion on such sensitive topics.

I note the UK government's Online Safety Bill, the legislation that policymakers claim will prevent online harms, contains just two mentions of the word 'education' in 145 pages.

We all have a role to play in supporting young people as they navigate online spaces. Prevention has been the key message for 15 years, but this approach isn't working. Young people are calling for education, delivered by people who understand the issues. This is not something that can be achieved by the platforms alone.

28 February 2022

The above information is reprinted with kind permission from The Conversation.
© 2010-2022, The Conversation Trust (UK) Limited

www.theconversation.com

The dark side of social media influencing

An article from *The Conversation*.

By Samira Farivar, Assistant Professor, Information Systems, Sprott School of Business, Carleton University, Fang Wang, Professor, Lazaridis School of Business and Economics, Wilfrid Laurier University, Ofir Turel, Professor, School of Computing and Information Systems, The University of Melbourne

THE CONVERSATION

Do you follow influencers on social media? Do you always check their posts? Do you find you're spending too much time or becoming obsessed with checking influencers' accounts? And when you can't check in, do you feel disconnected or lost?

If you answered yes to all of these questions, you may have whats known as 'problematic engagement' with social media influencers.

But don't blame yourself too much. You are among the many who have been swept away by dazzling social media influencing. And this can be attributed to many features and tactics social media influencers employ that help keep them influential — like livestreams and polls on Instagram.

As experts in social media and user behaviour, we recently published a paper that looks at followers' problematic engagement with influencers on social media. Our paper is among the first to study which aspects of social media influencing may lead to followers' problematic engagement. It is important to examine this context considering the significant volume and revenues of social media influencing — it's a US$13.8 billion industry.

The issue of problematic engagement

In the age of social media, most people know of or follow some social media influencers. Social media influencers are users who have a significant number of followers with established credibility.

Whether you are a fashion fan or want information on health and fitness — there's an influencer to follow. And followers often gravitate towards them for their authenticity and content creation.

But less focus is put on the dark side of social media influencing. Influencers are motivated and often incentivized (through product and brand endorsement) to increase their power on social media and many are becoming more proficient in attracting and engaging followers.

Followers, on the other hand, can easily become attached and obsessed with influencers and their engagement can often become excessive and unhealthy. Problematic engagement with social media influencers is common among followers, but not well known or understood.

Our research

We recently examined the factors and mechanisms that lead to problematic engagement. We focused on three influencer characteristics (physical attractiveness, social attractiveness and self-presence) and two follower participation attributes (participation comprehensiveness and following length) to explore their effects on the development of problematic engagement through the formation of follower attachments.

Based on attachment theory, we studied two types of attachments — parasocial relationship and sense of belonging, both of which are key in social media influencing. Parasocial relationship is followers' perception of their one-sided relationship with an influencer and sense of belonging refers to the feeling of being an integral member of the influencer's community.

We conducted an online survey of 500 Instagram users. The results showed that when followers develop attachments both to influencers (parasocial relationship) and their community (sense of belonging), this can lead to problematic engagement.

We found that influencers' social attractiveness has a stronger effect than other factors in building followers' attachments. Following more influencers could reduce the impact of attachment to the community (sense of belonging) when it comes to problematic engagement, but not the effect of attachment to the influencer (parasocial relationship).

Implications for influencers and followers

Our study warns of and explains problematic engagement to social media users.

We argue that social media users who are attracted to influencers can become easily attached and engage excessively. Users need to be aware of, watch out for and exert self-regulations to manage their interactions with influencers.

For example, participation comprehensiveness — which refers to the reasons for following and extent of followers' participation (like watching, liking, commenting, sharing)

— can lead to attachment development. This, however, can be consciously managed by followers themselves. One way of doing this is by making use of the phone's functions and tools like setting daily time limits on Instagram or turning off notifications for the app.

Social media influencers should also be aware of followers' problematic engagement. Although it may be in contrast with their goal of increasing follower engagement, they can focus on creating a healthy relationship with their followers.

For instance, influencers can openly talk about the issue of problematic engagement and show care for their followers' well-being. This will help with sustainability of the relationship because studies have shown that social media users with problematic behaviour are more likely to stop using platforms after a while.

More research on the dark side of social media influencers is needed and we call for future research to focus on additional negative consequences such as followers' anxiety, depression and the impact of following influencers on followers' well-being.

12 May 2022

The above information is reprinted with kind permission from The Conversation.
© 2010-2022, The Conversation Trust (UK) Limited

www.theconversation.com

Critical thinking online

The impact of online information.

We are influenced by everything around us, including the things we might come across online. Online information can impact our thoughts, feelings, beliefs and behaviour.

This includes:

♦ News articles

♦ Blog posts

♦ Nude or sexual photos

♦ Comments about the way people look

Some things we see online influence us in a positive way. For example, reading an article about someone starting a business might make us feel inspired.

Other things can influence us in a negative way. For example, something we read might make us believe something is real when it isn't. A video we watch might encourage us to behave dangerously or do things that could get us into trouble. Photos we see might make us think everyone else has the perfect body or life.

That's why it is important to be 'critically aware' of information online. Being critically aware involves being able to assess whether what we've read or seen is true and think about what impact it might have on us.

This can help us to decide whether or not we want to be influenced by the information.

'Fake news' (news or stories that are not true) spreads quickly and easily online. It can be hard to tell what's fake and what's real online. Fact-checking sites can help you to tell the difference between fact and fiction.

How to be critically aware of online information

There are some easy things you can do to increase your critical awareness of online information.

Assess it. Judge if you think things you see online have been edited to make people look better.

Check it. Look at another website or source of information that you know and trust to see if it backs up what you've read or seen.

Read it. Headlines or titles can be misleading. Read the whole article or blog carefully. Think about what they're saying and whether it seems true or not.

Speak to an adult you trust. They will be able to help you think about what you've seen, whether it's true or not and what impact it could have on you.

Being critically aware of people online

It is also important to be critically aware of people you meet online. Just like information we read or see online, they can influence how you behave or what you believe.

Before you are influenced by someone you have met online, you need to be sure they are who they say they are.

It is easy for people online to hide who they really are and pretend to be someone else. People who do this are sometimes called 'catfish'.

If you're worried that someone you've met online isn't who they say they are or if they are making you feel uncomfortable, speak to a trusted adult or report it to CEOP.

The above information is reprinted with kind permission from CEOP Education.
© Crown copyright 2022
This information is licensed under the Open Government Licence v3.0
To view this licence, visit http://www.nationalarchives.gov.uk/doc/open-government-licence/ **OGL**

www.thinkuknow.co.uk

Think before you post

People may behave differently online than they do in person - the large audience is invisible, so many feel protected by their screens. This can be a positive thing, like someone feeling more confident to open up and be themselves. But sometimes people will misuse social networks to shame and bully others.

Posting online is instant, public and more often than not, permanent. Once you post, you lose control of what happens to it - it only takes one friend to share it on their own profiles for it to be completely out of your hands..

The digital world is the real world with real consequences, so make sure you always ask yourself the following before you hit send!

Consider the following guidelines

Will I feel good or different about it later?

Social media comes with one golden rule, don't post when you are angry. A split second of rage can have permanent consequences.

Why am I posting?

Is this something you really want to post, does it really reflect your personality and values? Don't follow the crowd or post just to gain attention, as you might not like the response you get back.

Would I say this in person?

No? Then don't say it online. Social accounts are managed by real people with real feelings. If you talk about someone online, think about whether you would feel embarrassed or ashamed if you saw them in person. If so, you may want to ask again, why am I posting?

Can this be interpreted differently?

Sarcasm and irony do not often transfer well into writing, especially in a short social media post. Think about how others may read it; could it be seen as offensive?

Am I being kind?

Treat others with the respect that you would like to receive yourself. If you read it about yourself, would it make you feel good?

Is it really private?

People often excuse inappropriate posts based on the idea that the conversation is private, as it is on a private account. Consider how many connections you have, are all these people very close friends? Can you trust that each one of them won't share or talk about your post with others? Facebook statistics suggest that the average young user has up to 300 online friends. This private profile suddenly doesn't seem so private at all.

Do I have permission?

You might find that badly angled photograph of your friend amusing, but the likelihood is that they will not. Be respectful of other people's privacy; don't share photos or information that will embarrass or humiliate someone.

Would I like me?

If you were a stranger looking in at your profile, what would you think? If most of your posts are in some way critical, unkind, offensive or negative, how do you think you are being perceived?

Is it legal?

In the eyes of the law, posting online is not the same as having an informal chat with your friends. Posting is publishing, just the same as if it was written in the newspaper. Even if your profile is private, you do not own what you publish - meaning anyone can use it as evidence.

Make sure you do not post anything that might get you into trouble with the law. Harassment, hate speech, threats of violence, ruining someone's reputation and pictures or comments suggesting illegal activity can all be used against you.

The above information is reprinted with kind permission from Kidscape.
© Kidscape 2022

www.kidscape.org.uk

Be nice online and watch out for wokefishing: a Gen Z guide to dating as a teen

By Qais Hussain

For your average adult, dating is challenging, embarrassing, and confusing.

For teenagers, it's all the more so – with the added layer of toxicity that can come from happening mostly online.

The last decade has made online dating the norm, but in the pandemic, this intensified.

For many members of Gen Z, cooped up inside for the best part of their youth, meeting took place through sliding in the DMs, flirting through liked posts, and chats held via voice note.

Owen, an 18-year-old student, met his girlfriend of six months thanks to a DM slide.

'We had a lot of mutual friends on Instagram, and I long thought she looked pretty,' he tells Metro.co.uk. 'I messaged her, and we started talking for a bit.

'After a few weeks of messaging each other – we met up at a party, and after that, we became an item.'

Owen added: 'I am not going to lie; I would have never got a girlfriend if I didn't slide into her DMs. I would have been too scared to ask her in person.'

Psychotherapist Jack Worthy believes the rise of DM sliding is no bad thing.

'Courting evolves as technology evolves,' he tells us. 'Previous generations would pass notes in class or send mixtapes. Today, sliding into DMs is a modern evolution of expressing interest.'

So, how do you do the perfect DM slide?

First, you have to be connected with the person you're trying to 'link' with on social media; preferably Snapchat as you can tell when messages are being screenshotted and they don't save unless the recipient chooses to.

Don't go straight in with overly sexual chat. Keep it simple and friendly: ask them what they watch, what their hobbies are. Try the an open-ended question like: 'what was the last series you watched?'.

The key is not to get stuck for too long in the talking stage. While it's great to build a relationship online, make sure you're meeting in person at some point – try asking them if they fancy going out for a coffee, shisha or a bite to eat.

For young people dating online isn't just about using dating apps – it's about how relationships develop on social media and through private messaging.

Dating is considered a normal and often essential part of teen development, as more than a third of adolescents ages 13 to 17 have had some type of romantic experience. However, a survey in 2018 found that 21% of Gen Z-ers say

a texting conversation can count as a date. So many teens' interpretation of dating is different to what most of us assume.

But don't assume this makes our generation 'weird' – Worthy notes that plenty of teenage Gen X-ers spent hours on the phone with a love interest.

'Those interactions could feel like dates,' he says. 'Think of watching a movie with a boyfriend or girlfriend. You don't face one another. You don't interact. But we thought of those as dates.

'Texting together in real time can be a meaningful conversation.'

Many people assume that teenagers date just to release some lust, but for some, it's a way of reducing loneliness A report by The Mental Health Foundation found out that during the first lockdown, 35% of young people were experiencing loneliness. Online dating can be a solution.

Gemma is one of those teens who turned to online dating in lockdown.

'I was 16 and I was feeling incredibly isolated and lonely,' she tells Metro.co.uk. 'I didn't necessarily want to be in a romantic relationship with anyone, but I did want to get someone to talk to, and I wanted a friend.

'I joined a couple of friendship and dating apps, despite being underage for some of them, and I found company and friendship through that.'

'I was not put off with the fact that I was underage, I was cautious, of course; and in complete honestly, I didn't really discuss my age with anyone – I was simply on dating apps to keep busy.'

Again, that's not a bad thing. Worthy reckons that dating – online or off – is an important part of growing up.

He tells us: 'Learning to flirt, to read nonverbal cues, to negotiate consent, and metabolize rejection – these are all parts of becoming an adult and necessary for good mental health, regardless of the medium.'

Quick tips for dating as a teenager

Remember: safety first

If you meet anyone, make sure they are who they say they are (check various social media accounts), and meet in a public place, telling someone when and where you're meeting.

Don't forget your friends

It's easy to get swept up in romance, but don't ditch your mates for someone you fancy. Never forget your friends.

Remember the risks of sexting

An Ofsted report found that 80% of girls feel under pressure to send sexual images. Connecting with potential love interests online can be fun and exciting, and many teens feel the need to reveal the most intimate parts of their bodies; but remember that taking, sending, sharing, or having explicit photos of those under 18 is illegal – even if you're under 18, too.

Plus, in the wrong hands, a sext, can perpetuate bullying, emotional abuse, revenge porn, harassment, and embarrassment. Be extremely cautious.

Be nice online

Worthy encourages people to never behave online in a way they would not act in person. He says: 'The more removed you are from the person with whom you're communicating, the more likely your communication will be impersonal or insensitive or impulsive.

'We conduct ourselves differently over dating apps and social media (and usually worse) than in-person.'

Don't rush

It is difficult not to feel the pressure to move quickly into an intimate relationship, but just because 'everyone else is doing it' doesn't mean you have to.

Watch out for wokefishing

Wokefishing is a big problem for teenagers. To put it simply, this is where people parade progressive political views to get a swipe.

Given our strong political awareness, it's important for Gen Z-ers to know that the person they're dating isn't supporting causes in a performative way – they have to mean it.

6 March 2022

The above information is reprinted with kind permission from *Metro* & DMG Media Licensing.
© 2021 Associated Newspapers Limited

www.metro.co.uk

Chapter 2

Gaming

Gaming

In-game chat features allow you to connect with friends you know and new people from across the world.

Websites and apps outside of the game can also be used to speak to fellow gamers, organise online group games or get gaming tips and advice.

Gaming chat is exciting and creates a great sense of community when it's kept fun and positive.

Keeping the fun in online gaming

1. Be respectful and responsible. We all want to have a good time online, so it's important to treat each other with respect and kindness. Don't share any offensive content and respect each other's differences.

2. Play fair. A bit of competition is great, but it's not so fun when people aren't following the rules.

3. Keep it private. Don't give out any personal information that could identify you or your location. Consider what you share and remember to check your privacy settings.

Blocking and reporting

If someone makes you, or anyone else feel uncomfortable or upset, block or report them so they can't do it again.

When you block someone it normally means that although they can still send you messages, you will not receive them.

Sometimes blocking isn't enough. Some users should be reported to stop them from contacting other gamers too.

Report users that:

♦ Stalk, bully, discriminate against or abuse you or other users

♦ Are disruptive or threatening

♦ Put pressure on users to do things they're not comfortable with

♦ Share other users' and your own personal and account information

♦ Share or discuss sex or sexual content with under 18s

To find out how to block and report other users on specific games, visit their website.

4. Support other people. If you see someone else being bullied or pressured, be a positive bystander and do something about it. This could be seeking help or letting the person know you're there for them.

5. Speak to a trusted adult. If you come across something you aren't comfortable with, speak to a trusted adult or a support service like Childline. There are lots of people who can help if you or someone else are being bullied in a game.

What to look out for

It helps to be aware of some of the dangers so that you can get the best out of gaming online:

♦ Private chat. Nearly all platforms have in-game chat options, so you don't need to add gamer friends to private messaging apps like WhatsApp. Decline or ignore requests for private chats to avoid uncomfortable situations.

♦ People saying sexual things. It can be uncomfortable when someone online tries to talk to you about sex. Speak to a trusted adult or report it to CEOP so that they can support you if this happens.

♦ Requests for personal information. Other online gamers shouldn't be asking you for personal information. You don't have to tell anyone information about yourself, like where you go to school or where you live.

♦ Older gamers. Gamers come in all shapes and sizes so you're likely to connect with gamers of all ages. But it's strange for adults to try and get really close to you. Read our advice about relationships with older 'friends' and online grooming.

♦ Meeting up. Meeting someone you only know online or through a game is not always safe. Even if you have mutual friends, they could still be lying about who they are.

The above information is reprinted with kind permission from CEOP Education.
© Crown copyright 2022
This information is licensed under the Open Government Licence v3.0
To view this licence, visit http://www.nationalarchives.gov.uk/doc/open-government-licence/ **OGL**

www.thinkuknow.co.uk

4 Risks of online gaming

Online games are designed to be fun and an escape from the real world.

But there are some risks. Being aware of these will help you stay safe online and ensure you know when it's time to switch off.

Not everyone will be nice

Unfortunately, not everyone playing the game will be nice. Some gamers may say nasty or horrible things to you when you're playing, or may bully other players. Anyone can join the game, so you could be playing against someone you know or against a complete stranger (who might be a lot older than you).

Some gamers might not be who they say they are

Someone might start talking to you during the game and be really friendly. They may be trying to build your trust so they can trick you into doing something you don't want to do. If you're worried about online abuse or the way someone has been communicating online, you can report them to CEOP.

You might see things you don't like

The online game you are playing might have content or scenes that could upset you. This could be violence, horror, sex or murder. If you are playing virtual reality (VR) games, these scenes could be even more lifelike than if you were watching them in film.

You might not be able to stop playing

As online games have no end, you might find it hard to stop playing and start to become addicted. This could affect how much sleep you get at night, your concentration, and your results at school. It could also mean you lose friends if you stop seeing them.

How to get help

If you have any more questions on this area or would like to speak to somebody about this topic, have a look at the links below or search for your local services online.

Alternatively, you can always contact your school nurse.

♦ www.childline.org.uk/info-advice/bullying-abuse-safety/online-mobile-safety/online-gaming/

♦ www.familylives.org.uk/advice/teenagers/online/gaming/

♦ www.ceop.police.uk/Safety-Centre/

The above information is reprinted with kind permission from Health for Teens.
© 2022 Leicestershire Partnership NHS Trust

www.healthforteens.co.uk

Staying safe while gaming

One of the best things about online gaming is being able to do it with people all over the world. Meeting people through games can be really rewarding, as there is a guarantee you have at least a few things in common with them, and it's good to have people to play with that you've gotten to know in that space.

However, sometimes, not everyone is what they seem behind the screen. With online gaming, you never get the opportunity to actually see them, or really tell if what they are telling you is true. So we've put this together to help you identify some of the red flags of a catfish, or even a predator.

Ask yourself:

♦ Do they try to get personal information out of you, like how old you are, what your real name is, where you live and who you live with?

♦ Have they ever said anything to you that made you feel awkward or uneasy?

♦ Does something not quite add up in their stories they tell you?

♦ Do they refuse to speak over a headset, even though you and others have been using one?

♦ Are they weirdly somehow ALWAYS online when you log on?

♦ Have they ever pressured you to send pictures, or meet up in person?

♦ Are they sending you gifts for no reason?

If you are unsure:

♦ Talk to a trusted adult – whether it be a parent, older sibling or close friend. Talking about how you feel can really help make sense of your emotions and a situation.

♦ Ask the person why they need to know your personal information.

♦ Make your profile private, and deny friend requests from people you don't know.

♦ If they become persistent, block them on your chat platform. Even if it's only for a few days, give yourself time to reflect on what they are saying/asking.

♦ Trust your instincts, you don't have to say anything you don't want to. If something doesn't feel right to you, you don't have to reply.

How to protect yourself:

♦ Never give out personal information.

♦ Ensure your screen name does not contain personal information like your name or birthday.

♦ You could even come up with a cool name to use in games that's completely different to your real name.

♦ Keep a record of anything they do that makes you uncomfortable, you might need it in the future to report them.

♦ Report them as soon as you suspect they have bad intentions.

31 March 2022

The above information is reprinted with kind permission from Ditch the Label.
© 2022 Ditch the Label

www.ditchthelabel.org

The dark threats and sexual abuse women gamers endure

Polling finds 28 per cent of female gamers sexually harassed.

By Maya Oppenheim, Women's Correspondent

Not a day goes by, says Sunpi, a high-profile gamer, that a man she doesn't know sends her a dick pic, or asks if he can.

And the abuse she endures is often violent in its language. 'I've had people online harassing me saying they'll murder me and murder my family if I don't give them attention'.

The sexual abuse and sinister threats Sunpi has faced are sadly by no means unique. Women in gaming routinely suffer sexual harassment, aggressive abuse and sometimes even graphic threats of rape and murder from male gamers.

Research, shared exclusively with *The Independent,* found abuse experienced in the highly male-dominated world of gaming can often move on to social media and even translate into offline stalking and harassment.

The study, carried out by Young Gamers & Gamblers Education Trust (YGAM), discovered some 35 per cent of women said they have been sent inappropriate content or messages from other gamers. Some 28 per cent of female gamers have been sexually harassed by fellow gamers and 40 per cent verbally abused by gamers while playing online multiplayer games.

Almost three in 10 female gamers said they had been excluded from taking part in games due to their gender, and the majority of the 2,000 male and female gamers polled by the charity do not think enough is being done to tackle such toxic behaviour within gaming.

Sunpi, who streams on popular gaming site Twitch, said male gamers relentlessly comment on her appearance when she

is playing a game such as Fortnite or Call of Duty – adding that she is also bombarded with comments about her race.

'I am constantly sexualised,' she adds. 'They say: "You should make an OnlyFans". They don't say it to the men. They say: "Oh she is so exotic". Everything is always picked apart. The way I look. The way I put my leg out. I'm just trying to live without constantly being told I need to do porn. I'm told I'm being too sexual. I don't sit or stand right.'

Sunpi, who lives in the Midlands, said she regularly discovers innocuous clips of her simply sitting gaming fully-clothed have been uploaded to pornographic site Pornhub without her permission.

'I did a blog where I went to the gym and was playing Nintendo on the treadmill, while training, to promote a healthy lifestyle while gaming,' she recalls. 'A segment was taken out of the video and put on PornHub. I had to reach out and they removed it. Now I've got a point of contact to be like: "Hey can you please remove it?" as it happens a couple of times a month.'

Sunpi, who has a hefty online following on various social media platforms, said as well as being relentlessly objectified, people tell her she is a 'fake gamer' on a daily basis and that she is somehow not really playing games.

'They say I'm playing games for male attention,' Sunpi, who has been playing games since she can remember and now earns a living from gaming, adds. 'They say: "I don't believe this girl plays games". I'm a minority in gaming. I'm a mixed-race woman gamer.'

She said this week she received a message from a man offering her a £1,000 to send a naked video of herself farting, while others offer to pay her to meet up with them.

'Or they say, "If you let me send you dick pics, I will give you a £1,000,"' Sunpi adds. 'I'm not an item you can buy. I'm so used to it, I just think: 'Whatever, it is what it is'. I would never give up gaming because of this harassment. The positive feedback from my followers is why I do it.'

But the horrific repercussions of such online abuse transcend the computer or mobile screen and can translate into real-world danger – with Sunpi recounting when a gamer stalked her and tried to work out where she lived.

'Being online can be so stressful because of those reasons,' she adds. 'It makes me sometimes feel a bit insecure within myself. All the time I question the way I dress. Also sometimes I feel stressed and overwhelmed. Recently a brand told me I was too risky. If you look at the content on my Instagram, it is not risky.'

In February, a female gamer, 19-year-old Ingrid Oliveira Bueno da Silva, was found murdered in Brazil, allegedly at the hands of a male rival gamer.

Bryter, a market research company that carries out annual polls on female gamers, discovered an average of 10 per cent of female gamers received rape threats between 2018 and 2020.

Jay-Ann Lopez, the founder of Black Girl Gamers, tells women gamers endure a great deal of 'vitriol' online – with people hurling 'racist and sexist epithets' at them.

'I get emails with the n-word, or where I'm called a monkey, or a racist, or a race-baiter, or a lot of comparisons to gorillas,' she adds. 'As a lighter-skinned black woman who is slim, I don't experience some of the negativity to a lot of body shapes. Most women I know have experienced some kind of sexism or sexualised comments to them in gaming.'

Ms Lopez, who founded the popular gaming collective in 2015, said male gamers had told her 'women should belong in the kitchen' and have demanded she make them a sandwich.

Last summer, more than 70 people in the gaming industry – who were predominantly women – went public with allegations of sexism, gender-based harassment and sexual assault via Twitch, Twitter and other social media platforms.

Molly Barker, a 21-year-old student who lives in London, said she hasn't gamed online for years after facing abuse from men when she was younger.

'It's just not even worth going online,' Ms Barker, who studies Psychology and Cognitive and Clinical Neuroscience at Royal Holloway University, says. 'If a man feels outclassed by a woman in a game then he is more likely to abuse her. Lower to medium level players are more likely to abuse.'

She said when she streamed on Twitch men messaged asking to buy nudes, and when she has voiced opinions on gaming on Twitter, she has had people say: 'Shut up I'll hurt you'.

'It was just for having an opinion on a video game,' she adds. 'Gaming is meant to be an escape. Gaming is about not thinking about things. But it allows people to abuse anonymously. It makes them more emboldened. It gives people an anonymous platform to spew toxicity.'

6 June 2021

The above information is reprinted with kind permission from *The Independent*.
© independent.co.uk 2022

www.independent.co.uk

How much of your time is screen time?

We reveal what percentage of our lives we spend looking at screens and the effects it has on our wellbeing.

By Catherine Hiley, Senior Content Editor

Most of us will have received the dreaded Screen Time notification telling us how much time we've spent on our phones in the last week.

Research has revealed that in 2020 the average adult spent three hours a day on social media, in comparison to only 90 minutes in 2012. Further research has shown that spending too much time on your mobile phone can contribute to mental health issues.

We have looked into what percentage of our lives we spend glued to the screen and what effects this can have on our wellbeing.

UK adults spend half of every day in front of a screen

While social media isn't new (remember Myspace and Bebo?) the UK's addiction to the platforms really took hold over the last decade. The decade that brought us Instagram, Pinterest and Snapchat amongst others.

Our study reveals that in 2010, 51% of males and 56% of females aged between 16 - 24 had created at least one social media account. In comparison, in 2019 78% of males and 86% of females of the same age had a social media profile. The growth in these percentages demonstrates the younger generations' reliance on social media media that has become a staple in everyday life.

Social media has become a vital means of staying connected, whether we're communicating on Facebook Messenger or using Tinder and Hinge to meet new people. These days, most new conversations don't start by picking up the phone for a call, instead asking someone for their Instagram or Snapchat handle.

Our study reveals that the average UK citizen spends up to 6.4 hours a day on the internet using any device, which is nearly the same amount of time as an average shift at work. In addition, the study shows that UK adults spend on average four hours a day watching TV, which is 1,350 hours per year! UK adults spend almost half of the day in front of the screen, browsing the internet and watching television.

The gender split on social media

Based on the number of profiles created in the UK between 2010-2019

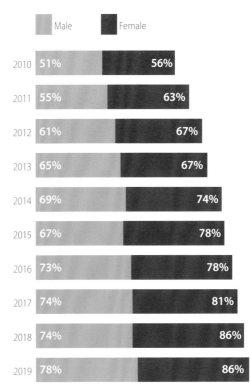

	Male	Female
2010	51%	56%
2011	55%	63%
2012	61%	67%
2013	65%	67%
2014	69%	74%
2015	67%	78%
2016	73%	78%
2017	74%	81%
2018	74%	86%
2019	78%	86%

Source: Uswitch

Average screen time per day

Listening to music
75 min
420 hrs per year

Watching TV
241 min
1,350 hrs per year

Using social media
109 min
610 hrs per year

Using the internet
386 min
2,162 hrs per year

Source: Uswitch

In addition, we spend 1.8 hours a day on social media and 1.3 hours listening to music, totalling that UK adults are spending on average 4,542 hours in front of a screen each year.

Brits watch nearly 1,000 hours of TV every year

Sitting in front of the TV watching the news or the latest soap has been a staple in British culture since the 1950s. From live TV, streaming, gaming and YouTube to watching on demand, there are so many ways we consume television.

Despite the growth in streaming, live TV still holds its weight against the big streaming services, such as Netflix and Amazon Prime. Our data reveals that Brits spend up to 21 hours a week watching live TV, which is equivalent to 997 hours a year!

A 2017 study from TV Licensing found the main public service broadcast channels (BBC1, BBC2, ITV/STV/UTV, Channel 4 and Channel 5) held half of the total broadcast TV audience despite the growing list of choices consumers have today.

In second place is streaming, with UK adults spending 71 minutes per day using SVod services, equivalent to 398 hours per year. The TV Licensing study also found that in 2016 BBC iPlayer was the most popular streaming service among adults, with 61% of respondents saying they use it.

The study also revealed that 38% of respondents watched YouTube, with UK adults spending 48 minutes per day on the site - that's 269 hours a year. Time spent watching YouTube has surpassed more traditional mediums, such as recorded playback and DVDs.

Americans spend on average 325 hours a year on Facebook

Social networks have revolutionised how we communicate with one another. Long gone are the days where you would need a landline or Yellow Pages to communicate. 85% of Americans have a smartphone with its main use to communicate through social media apps.

The study reveals that Americans are spending 35 minutes on average a day using social media, which is 195 hours a year. The biggest culprit in grabbing American's attention is Facebook, with US users spending on average 58 minutes a day on the app, which is 325 hours a year!

Coming in at second is Instagram. The image sharing network is popular amongst Gen-Z and it's not hard to see why so many Americans get sucked into scrolling through their feed for extensive periods of time. Americans are spending up to 53 minutes a day on these apps, which is equivalent to up to 297 hours a year.

We might not pay close attention to how much time we spend scrolling on our phones due to the endless news feeds that apps have today. But studies have shown that screen time releases dopamine to the brain which can negatively affect impulse control and,make screen time very addictive.

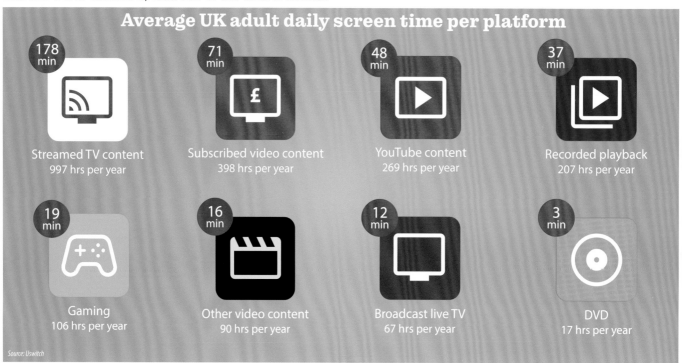

Average UK adult daily screen time per platform

178 min
Streamed TV content
997 hrs per year

71 min
Subscribed video content
398 hrs per year

48 min
YouTube content
269 hrs per year

37 min
Recorded playback
207 hrs per year

19 min
Gaming
106 hrs per year

16 min
Other video content
90 hrs per year

12 min
Broadcast live TV
67 hrs per year

3 min
DVD
17 hrs per year

Source: Uswitch

Americans are guilty of scrolling on social media and watching TV at the same time

With access to thousands of TV shows and movies ready to binge at our fingertips, research reveals that 74% of Americans are signed up to a streaming service. While we might think we're paying attention to the latest episode of Stranger Things or true crime drama, many of us are often scrolling on our phones at the same time.

Our study shows that Americans are spending similar amounts of time watching TV (3.29 hours) and on their mobile (3.49 hours) per day. According to Neilsen, many use their mobiles as an extension of entertainment. 71% of subjects from Neilsen's study said they used their smartphone to find out more information about what they're watching, 41% said they use devices to send messages about what they're watching, and 28% said they used social-media apps to read and write posts during the show.

Our study also revealed which American states spend the most time on screens, with Arizona coming in first place with an average of 4.6 hours per day or 1,546 hours per year. This is closely followed by Connecticut and Nevada with 4.4 hours per day, equivalent to four episodes of Game of Thrones or 12 episodes of The Simpsons. The state with the lowest screen time was Alabama whose residents consumed only 1.8 hours a day, followed by Vermont (2.1 hours) and Oklahoma (2.2 hours).

Gen-Z are spending a shocking nine hours per day in front of a screen

Since its launch in 2010, Instagram has gained one billion active users and is one of the most popular apps amongst Gen-Z. Our study reveals that its users are predominantly the ages 13-17 (6.8%), 18-24 (25.30%) and 25-34 (30.90%).

Facebook has seen a decline in users over the past few years especially in the younger demographic, with studies showing that 65% of Gen-Z check Instagram on a daily basis in comparison to 35% who do the same on Facebook. The younger generation is gravitating towards apps like Instagram and TikTok, as they allow them to be more creative and express themselves. Facebook is often seen as the place you'll find your parents.

Our study has revealed that kids aged between 5-16 are spending up to nine hours a day in front of screens. A report by Commonsense Media revealed that the percentage of Gen-Z who say they watch online videos every day has more than doubled since 2015, from 24% to 56% among 8-12 year olds, and from 34% to 69% among 13-18 year olds.

Despite the boom in television content, the study reveals that tweens and teens are spending less time watching TV on a traditional television set. The percentage who say they enjoy watching TV has dropped from 61% to 50% among tweens, and from 45% to 33% for teens, over the past four years. Our study reveals that kids are spending the same amount of time on the internet as they are watching television, which suggests that they are doing this simultaneously.

Too much screen time can have effects on mental and physical health

While we might enjoy watching the latest vlog, calling friends on FaceTime or posting to Instagram, spending too much time staring at a screen does have a downside. There is a big correlation between screen time and its effects on health.

Too much time in front of the screen can have adverse health effects, from weight gain and poor sleep to increased susceptibility to certain diseases. The increase in screen time goes hand in hand with sedentary behaviour, which in turn could lead to poorer physical health and wellbeing. In addition, the constant use of screens has a negative effect on sleep for children and young people, which is vital for good wellbeing and health.

Numerous studies reveal that extensive periods of screen time can lead to depression and anxiety. With the growth of social media apps comes unrealistic standards that are portrayed on these apps to show the "perfect" life. These comparisons can lead to negative thoughts, low self esteem and confidence issues. Studies have shown that adults who watched TV or used a computer for more than six hours per day were more likely to experience moderate to severe depression.

Tips to reduce your screen time

While many might be conscious of how much time they're spending in front of screens thanks to Screen Time notifications, being surrounded by constant entertainment is addictive. Here are some tips to help reduce your screen time and its effects:

- Go easy on the eyes and turn on dark mode.

- Make a note of how much time you're spending in front of a screen and make a consistent effort to reduce your screen time. This can be done by implementing a no phones before bed rule, setting a time limit on social media apps through your phone's settings so you can't access them or going on a walk at lunch time rather than scrolling.

- Take on a new hobby, whether you've always wanted to become the next Bob Ross at painting or you'd like to try out a new fitness class at the gym, it's the perfect way to get away from the screen for an hour.

- Take a digital detox by substituting your usual binge watching with spending more time with friends or getting creative in the kitchen.

Methodology

Using data collated from OfCom, Statista, NHSGGC and Broadband Search, we've looked into the percentage of our time spent in front of screens and what effects this can have on wellbeing.

15 June 2021

The above information is reprinted with kind permission from Uswitch.
© 2000-2022 Uswitch Limited

www.uswitch.com

What happens psychologically when we're cut off from social media?

The social media outage proved just how addictive these apps can be.

By Prudence Wade

In what is being called the 'great social media blackout of 2021', for more than five hours on October 4, the impossible happened: Facebook, Instagram and WhatsApp all went down.

For so many of us heavily reliant on social media and messaging sites to entertain ourselves and communicate with friends and family, it was something close to a nightmare.

Facebook blamed a 'faulty configuration change' for the outage which caused a 'cascading effect' bringing platforms to a halt, and while it's now fixed, it was a sharp reminder of how dependent we are on social media.

Many of us rushed to other platforms such as Twitter to get our fix, and even resorted to (gasp) actually texting or calling our friends.

'What's really interesting with the outage is the immediate digital detox that we were all forced to engage with that wasn't voluntary,' says Dr Rachael Kent, lecturer in digital economy and society at King's College London and founder of Dr Digital Health.

'We're all now grappling day-to-day with managing our digital nutrition and our digital habits, trying to have healthier relationships with our tech [so it's] not to be too addictive and compulsive.

'However with the outage we were forced immediately to stop reaching for our phones, or even if we were reaching

for our phone, not getting that dopamine kick, and that entertainment and sociality from the device that we are so used to having so readily available at our disposal whenever we want it.'

This showed just how addicted many of us are to social media. 'It was hugely challenging and immediately forced us to not only have a digital detox, but also confront our addictive relationship with not only our phones, but also the applications themselves,' explains Kent.

If you're a habitual user of Facebook, Instagram or WhatsApp, you might have found yourself constantly opening the apps, only to remember they were down.

For Kent, this relationship 'really illustrates how much they'd have become an extension of our physicality, as a mediating tool to enable so much: community, connection, communication, sociality. The inability to stop picking it up despite the fact that you know it's not working really illustrates that dependence.'

This forced hiatus might have stirred up some negative emotions – particularly for businesses running on these platforms.

'On the business front, there's always going to be a lot of anxiety around not being able to manage and run your business effectively,' Kent explains. 'We live in an always-on, always-available culture that was immediately halted.'

She suggests the average user of the apps would have also experienced 'anxiety, but for different reasons – the inability to be able to scroll, doom scroll or habitually scroll, to not be able to access products and services you might want to buy, as well as not being able to chat with one's friends.'

Kent hopes the outage will cause us to re-evaluate our relationships with these addictive apps.

'I would like to think it forced us to think, what can I do to entertain myself? How can I communicate with friends and family without using these platforms? And also forced us to think about non-digital analogue methods of entertainment, so reading a book, journaling, cooking a meal, for example,' she says.

In an ideal world, the outage will cause us to have a healthier online life, but 'the reality of that?' she asks, 'I don't know how long that will last.'

5 October 2021

The above information is reprinted with kind permission from *The Independent*.
© independent.co.uk 2022

www.independent.co.uk

6 Signs you need a digital detox, as Rylan Clark-Neal returns to twitter

The presenter took a five-month break from the social media site.

By Katie Wright

After a break of more than five months, Rylan Clark-Neal has returned to Twitter. The presenter split from his husband Dan Neal earlier this summer and said he was focusing on his mental health.

'So…. What did I miss?' the 32-year-old asked his 1.6m followers in his first tweet since April.

In July, Clark-Neal released a statement saying he and his husband were 'currently prioritising our mental health and looking after the ones around us we love most.'

He added: 'I am working towards getting back to the jobs I love in due course. Thank you for being patient with me.'

It's encouraging to see a celebrity speaking openly about the negative side of social media and the need to recognise when it may be time to have a digital detox. So, whether you've been through a break up or just need to focus on your mental health without a constant stream of social media adding to your stress and anxiety, here's when you might want to consider a break too.

1. Your phone is the first thing you look at in the morning

Do you immediately grab your phone the minute you wake up to check your emails, reply to Whatsapp messages or scroll Instagram? The same way some people crave caffeine, your brain may be hooked on the dopamine buzz you get every time you see a notification on your phone.

2. …and the last thing at night

Sleep experts say that we should avoid screens of all kinds for an hour before bed, as the blue light they emit can prevent you from falling asleep.

If you find yourself messing around on your phone in bed or even checking it when you wake up during the night, you might want to consider turning it off completely or banning devices from the bedroom and using an alarm clock instead.

3. You procrastinate too much

There's nothing wrong with taking breaks, catching up on messages or sharing funny memes, but when you use certain sites to scroll mindlessly and put off work or essential tasks it can really affect your productivity. App blocks can be really useful for helping you stop procrastinating.

4. You're never 'in the moment'

Like a music fan viewing an entire concert through their phone screen, if you're constantly thinking 'This would make an amazing Instagram post' instead of enjoying that delicious meal/beautiful sunset/cute puppy, chances are you're not living 'in the moment'. A digital detox can help you be more mindful and appreciate the little things in life.

5. It's affecting your mental health

Social media can be a source of fun and a great way to keep in touch with loved ones, but if scrolling on Instagram makes you feel anxious or depressed because you're comparing yourself to the heavily filtered and edited versions of friends, influencers or celebrities it's not good for your mental health.

Similarly, if getting in arguments about politics with family members on Facebook leaves you feeling angry and frustrated, it's time to take a step back and remember that you don't have to engage with – or even look at – their posts if you don't want to.

6. People say 'You're always on your phone'

Sometimes, we don't even realise how detrimental our digital habits are until someone else points it out. If friends or family have complained that you're always glued to your smartphone, you may be missing out on quality time and real-life connections. A digital detox could be what you need to break the cycle and stop you being so dependent on your device.

17 September 2021

The above information is reprinted with kind permission from *The Independent*.
© independent.co.uk 2022

www.independent.co.uk

Key Facts

- In 2021, 4.33 billion people worldwide were using social media. (page 2)

- The world's population is currently sat at around 7.9 billion. (page 2)

- People aged between 35 and 49 make up the largest demographic of Twitter users – 28.4 per cent of the total usage population. (page 3)

- On average, a rather sizeable 500 million tweets are shared per day. This works out at 6,000 tweets per second, 350,000 tweets per minute, and a whopping 200 billion tweets every year. (page 3)

- About 16% of three- and four-year-olds view TikTok content.(page 4)

- UK data shows, girls experience a negative link between social media use and life satisfaction when they are 11-13 years old and boys when they are 14-15 years old. (page 5)

- Six in ten children aged 8-17 who used social media or any messaging/ voice/ video calling apps/ sites felt that these types of platforms made them feel happy (59%) or closer to their friends (61%) all or most of the time. (page 10)

- Eight in ten children aged 8-17 (78%) said they had felt, at some point, that people could be mean or unkind to each other on social media. (page 10)

- The majority of 8-17s who use social media thought that only some of what they see on social media is true (63%). However, one in ten believed that everything they see on social media is true (12%). (page 10)

- A third of children aged 8-17 who use apps and sites for school or homework believed that everything they saw on these apps or sites was true. (page 11)

- Three-quarters of children aged 12-17 claimed to be confident in their ability to judge what is real and what is fake online. (page 11)

- When shown a fake social media profile, more than a fifth of 12-17s identified a fake profile as a genuine one. (page 12)

- More than a third of children aged 8-17 had encountered worrying or nasty content online. (page 13)

- The name 'metaverse' isn't actually that new: it first appeared in a dystopian 1992 novel, Snow Crash, by the sci-fi writer Neal Stephenson. (page 18)

- Facebook has committed to hiring 10,000 highly specialised engineers based in the EU over the next five years to build Meta. (page 20)

- 21% of Gen Z-ers say a texting conversation can count as a date. (page 29)

- 35 per cent of women said they have been sent inappropriate content or messages from other gamers. (page 33)

- Almost three in 10 female gamers said they had been excluded from taking part in games due to their gender. (page 33)

- in 2020 the average adult spent three hours a day on social media, in comparison to only 90 minutes in 2012. (page 35)

- in 2010, 51% of males and 56% of females aged between 16 - 24 had created at least one social media account. In comparison, in 2019 78% of males and 86% of females of the same age had a social media profile. (page 35)

- the average UK citizen spends up to 6.4 hours a day on the internet. (page 35)

- Since its launch in 2010, Instagram has gained one billion active users and is one of the most popular apps amongst Gen-Z. (page 37)

Blog

A website which features individual writers' or groups of writers' personal discourse (similar to a journal), sharing ideas, information, opinions and observations. Entries are added regularly and may feature photos, videos and interactive comments left by readers.

Catfishing

A type of impersonation involving stealing someone's identity and posing as them to deceive others.

CEOP

Child Exploitation and Online Protection - CEOP helps keep young people safe from online grooming and sexual abuse.

Cyberbullying

Cyberbullying is when technology is used to harass, embarrass or threaten to hurt someone. A lot is done through social networking sites such as Facebook and Twitter. Bullying via mobile phones is also a form of cyberbullying. With the use of technology on the rise, there are more and more incidents of cyberbullying.

Digital abuse

Most frequently occurring in teenage relationships, digital abuse involves the use of texting and social networking sites to keep track of, harass, stalk, control, bully or intimidate a partner.

Digital detox

A period of time where a social networking user spends away from using social media. This is often to break the habit or addiction that some experience from using social media. Some people will also try to avoid all forms of digital communication, such as email or instant messaging in this time too.

Digital footprint

The 'trail' a person leaves behind when they interact with the digital environment. This evidence left behind gives clues as to the person's existence, presence and identity. It also refers to what other people may say about you online, not just yourself: sometimes also referred to as your online presence.

Digital native

A person who has grown up surrounded by digital technology, such as mobile phones, computers and the Internet (the current 12- to 18-year-old generation).

Hashtag (#)

The hashtag symbol (#) goes in front of a word or phrase to identify the topic of that message. This is commonly used on social networking sites, such as Twitter. On Twitter, when a hashtag rapidly becomes popular this is referred to as a 'trending topic'.

Internet

A worldwide system of interlinked computers, all communicating with each other via phone lines, satellite links, wireless networks and cable systems.

Parental control software/Network-level filters

Parental control software makes use of web filters to block access to certain websites that contain inappropriate content for minors. This includes websites about suicide/self-harm, gambling, file sharing and pornography. Net-filters provide parents with the option of blocking adult content, such as porn, and placing certain websites on a 'black list' so that they cannot be accessed. In 2012, the four leading Internet service providers in the UK (BT, Sky, TalkTalk and Virgin) will offer new customers the choice of whether or not they want to turn on parental control software.

Screen time

A term used to refer to the amount of time someone (usually young children) spend in front of a screen. For example, a tablet, smartphone or computer.

Social media

Media which are designed specifically for electronic communication. 'Social networking' websites allow users to interact using instant messaging, share information, photos and videos and ultimately create an online community. Examples include Facebook, LinkedIn and micro-blogging site Twitter.

Social media addiction

This addiction means spending an increasing amount of time on social media, taking time away from other daily tasks. Those that are addicted experience unpleasant feelings if they cannot access their social media for any period of time. It can also affect people's sleep, as they often wake during the night to check their social media accounts.

Social networking sites

A place online where people, usually with similar interests, hobbies or backgrounds, can build social networks and social relations together. Examples include websites such as Facebook, Twitter and Pinterest.

Troll/Troller/Trolling

Troll is Internet slang for someone who intentionally posts something online to provoke a reaction. The idea behind the trolling phenomenon is that it is about humour, mischief and, some argue, freedom of speech; it can be anything from a cheeky remark to a violent threat. However, sometimes these Internet pranks can be taken too far, such as a person who defaces an Internet tribute site, causing the victim's family further grief.

Activities

Brainstorming

♦ In small groups, discuss what you know about social networking. Consider the following points:

· What are the different types of social networks?

· What are the different types of social media?

· How many do you use on a daily basis?

· What is a digital footprint?

♦ In small groups, create a list of pros and cons for using social media.

♦ In pairs, discuss the signs and symptoms of social media addiction. Feedback to your class.

♦ In small groups, list as many social networking sites as you can.

Research

♦ Do you know what your digital footprint is? Type your name into a search engine and see what information you can find about yourself. Has this changed the way you view Internet privacy/security?

♦ Design a questionnaire that will evaluate how much time people spend on social media daily. Distribute the questionnaire to your classmates as well as friends and family. Create a report on your findings. Take into account the differences between age groups and genders.

♦ Do some research to find out about positive, unusual and innovative uses for social media. Write some notes and feedback to your class.

♦ Do some research on the minimum user age that social media sites have. Which sites have the lowest and highest ages?

♦ Design a questionnaire to evaluate how social media makes people feel. Then feedback to your class. Consider the following:

· Pressure to reply to messages – as many people use 'read receipts' on WhatsApp or iMessage you can often see that someone has read your message but not yet replied.

· Pressure to complete a 'Snapchat Streak' – If you lose the streak do you lose a friendship? Is it important to validate a friendship?

· FOMO – How does the fear of missing out affect people? Does this encourage them to carry on using social media?

Design

♦ Design a social networking app that would be suitable for children under 13 to use. Consider features such as security, privacy and parental controls.

♦ Choose one of the articles from this book and create an illustration for it.

♦ Design a leaflet with tips on how to digitally detox.

♦ Create a poster on how to deal with cyberbullying.

♦ Create an infographic using one of the articles on this topic.

♦ Design a poster on how to game safely.

♦ Design a poster on how to report upsetting/unwanted activity online.

Oral

♦ Are social networking sites beneficial or can they be harmful? Debate this question as a class.

♦ In small groups, create a presentation that explains the concept of digital detoxing. Your presentation should be aimed at 11-year-old pupils, and should offer advice on how to reduce your time online.

♦ In small groups, create a short radio advert that promotes 'Scroll Free September'.

♦ As a class, debate the minimum age requirements that social networking sites stipulate. One half of the class should be against a minimum age, and the other in favour.

♦ In pairs, discuss ways to stay safe online.

Reading/writing

♦ Watch The Circle (2017) (12). How does this film portray the topic of social media? Do you think this is a realistic portrayal? Do you think that social media may develop this way in the future? Write a short story using the film and your thoughts on it as inspiration.

♦ Imagine that you are an agony aunt/uncle and you have had a letter from a teen who is being cyberbullied. Write a reply to them telling them how they can get help.

♦ Write an email to your parents/carers to try and persuade them to use social media less.

♦ 'Children should be taught social networking skills at school.' Do you agree or disagree with this statement? Write 500 words exploring your answer.

Index

Acknowledgements

The publisher is grateful for permission to reproduce the material in this book. While every care has been taken to trace and acknowledge copyright, the publisher tenders its apology for any accidental infringement or where copyright has proved untraceable. The publisher would be pleased to come to a suitable arrangement in any such case with the rightful owner.

The material reproduced in **issues** books is provided as an educational resource only. The views, opinions and information contained within reprinted material in **issues** books do not necessarily represent those of Independence Educational Publishers and its employees.

Images

Cover image courtesy of iStock. All other images courtesy Freepik, Pixabay & Unsplash.

Illustrations

Simon Kneebone: pages 26, 27 & 31. Angelo Madrid: pages 2, 18 & 32.

Additional acknowledgements

With thanks to the Independence team: Shelley Baldry, Tracy Biram, Klaudia Sommer and Jackie Staines.

Danielle Lobban

Cambridge, June 2022